For My Eyes Only

An Interactive Pathway to Improve Your
Health and Happiness

For My Eyes Only

*An Interactive Pathway to Improve Your
Health and Happiness*

A. Henri Moyal, M.D.

Published by A. Henri Moyal

A. Henri Moyal, Publisher

Dedication

This book is dedicated to the memory of my parents--despite their apprehension regarding my pursuits in the magical field of psychiatry; to my two dear sons and my ever-turbulent grandchildren with all my love; to Dr. Wulsin, my first and most important psychiatric instructor, with my deepest and everlasting appreciation; and to each and every patient who gave me the honor of entering their lives and learning from them.

Acknowledgments

I gratefully acknowledge my two sons, Laurent and Michael, for strongly encouraging me to write down my thoughts, and actually work on this project; my young assistant, Brie Ann Lundell, for being my first critic, coach, and reviewer; my dear cousin, Lynda Brunisholz-Moyal, for configuring and putting order to the first, second and third drafts; my co-worker and unofficial editor, Carrie Freeland, for her honest opinions, reviews, and corrections of the penultimate draft; Stan Witt, who served as my project advisor; Michelle Witt, for special assistance in creating the section entitled "Coping Skills"; Simon Tsosie, for book cover design, formatting, and graphics; and many of my co-workers, for encouraging me to write the self-scoring inventory and the interactive response section dealing with improving one's success in improving health and happiness.

Learn from yesterday
Live for today
Hope for tomorrow
The important thing is to not stop questioning.

--Albert Einstein

Preface

If you have ever played chess or watched chess players, you probably know that the King is the most vital piece in the game. The game is over and lost when the King is captured or unable to make any more moves.

In your own life, you are like the King. And, as with chess, you have many abilities to help you become a winner. You and your opponent, you must also recognize, possess an equal number of imperfections that can prevent either of you from achieving your personal royal goals.

For My Eyes Only gives you the opportunity to reflect on significant factors and experiences in your past. You will be able to see how they have affected you over the years. You will also be able to analyze how much your life has changed for better or worse and how your current life has been influenced by your previous experiences—or, to use our metaphor—by your previous moves on the chess board of life. Finally, you can plan a meaningful future based on your analysis—and, consequently, you can dwell more happily on the chess board of life.

Finally, when looking forward to a meaningful future, you have the opportunity to focus on the years to come and decide what your aspirations, wishes, and projects can or should be used on the chess board of life.

In the three time dimensions (past, present, and future) and through 13 or 14 parameters, you will develop a clear and objective view of many significant events in your life and realize how much you have actually accomplished over the years. You will also see how much more you expect or wish to achieve in the years to come.

For My Eyes Only is not designed to negatively portray or criticize any of your past or present life experiences. Rather, it is designed to help you reflect on your current achievements and to look forward to more positive and substantial improvements in some special areas of your life.

In time, your various scores that you obtain with respect to the three time dimensions can be shared with your significant partner or certain family members in order to reach a mutual understanding of the person you once were, are presently, and aspire to become.

Please realize that this interactive self-study is designed for you to re-score yourself periodically, on the forms provided, *to see how your perceptions of past events and future goals evolve over time. These changes in perception can both delight and call your attention to areas needing further improvement. In this sense, For My Eyes Only* can be a valuable friend and guide for many years.*

*For My Eyes Only will soon be published in eBook form; thus, eBook readers may do their scoring in a Journal that can be purchased at an office supply.

CONTENTS

Part One
The Fourteen Dimensions

~

£

Part Two
Aristotle Modernized:
Constituent Elements of Health
and Happiness

~

Part Three
Coping Skills and Strategies for Obtaining Health and Happiness

~

The Importance of Coping Skills and Strategies
Personalizing Coping Skills to Improve Your Life
When Do You Ask For Professional Help?
Appreciate Your Progress
Coping Skills Work Sheets

£

Post Script
£

Part One
The Fourteen Dimensions
£

Your Pathway to Health and Happiness

Part One is divided into two major divisions. The first division consists of 13 for all participants (and for some, 14) as well as parameters that will help you to survey your entire life and to evaluate past and present experiences, significant events, traumas, and short and long term wishes and expectations for the years to come.

Earlier it was mentioned that For My Eyes Only is a program that will help you to develop a more objective view of your past and present; this volume will also help give you a clear idea about how far you are from reaching your future goals. It will assist you to focus on areas or dimensions that you will need to change in order to reach those goals.

While following this program, you will be asked to score yourself on many dimensions or topics. These scores will then be entered into a graph. You will start by analyzing your past so you can see your starting point. You will then have the option to analyze your Present on the same 13 or 14 dimensions. The last step will be analyzing your future – which is where you would like to be on each dimension in the future. After completing your scoring, you may be interested in comparing your scores to the established score ranges contained in this book.

It is recommended that you re-score yourself occasionally throughout your life. Your scores may be months or even years apart depending on significant events or changes in your current life, be they positive or negative.

One would expect that Past scores should not change much over time since we cannot change the past. However, when you reevaluate your PAST scores, you may be surprised to see that some scores change as your perception of some past experiences have changed. By the same token, your Present and Future scores may change over time. Present situations change throughout life and Future goals are often modified. It will therefore be helpful to write down the date each time you score yourself in order to have a more concrete idea of the changes you go through over time. That will be an easy way to realize how much you have accomplished since your past and how far you are from reaching your personal future goals.

In Division Two, you will again be scoring your current life – but this time according to Aristotle's five principles in the pursuit of inner peace, harmony, and personal happiness.

What will these average scores tell you? Each number will give you a visual representation of how you perceive different segments of your life. A score with the maximum value means that everything is wonderful. A very low score means that you have a lot to work on to achieve a sense of fulfillment and happiness.

The goal of any self-help book such as this one is to show you where you are today yet also give you a clear picture of where you want to be in the future. As with the PAST, so the PRESENT section can be used time and time again over the following years. When you come back to these assessments after you have implemented some coping strategies to help improve your quality of life, you will witness how the scores have changed over time. Some may be higher while some may be lower as your priorities change with age and maturity.

As with all these evaluation tools, there are no right or wrong answers. There are no magic tools to suddenly make your life more meaningful or peaceful. That being said, by knowing what you experienced in the past, where you are now, and especially where you would like to be, you will be better prepared to make changes in the direction of better health and greater happiness.

3

Preliminary Definitions: PAST, PRESENT, and FUTURE

PAST refers to significant events or people in previous years that affect who they are today. You can choose what period of your past you wish to evaluate. It could be a few years or many decades back in your life, depending on your age and when some significant changes occurred. It may be helpful to write down what time period you are scoring for each dimension (i.e. early childhood, teens, early 20s, etc.).

PRESENT refers to our current life, although this time period could be extended back to the last couple of years.

FUTURE will, of course, depend on your current age. Since most people are not aware of their personal life expectancy, they are free to set goals to reach within 5 years or even as far as 30-to-50 years from the present. Again, it may be helpful to write down what time period <u>you are scoring for each dimension for future reference.</u>**

**For each of the 14 dimensions, the total score may be the sum of multiple partial scores OR it may reflect your overall impression or experience. The scoring that is not to be added is used to serve as a reminder of the events or issues at that time in your life. Follow scoring instructions carefully for each dimension.

Explanation of Dimension One: Family and Friends

PAST:

Health and traumas are only 2 of many possible significant issues through which family and friends may have influenced and affected your memories of your past.

What was the overall impact that your interaction with family and friends had on you? Score each line up to 5 lines if relevant, with their overall influence, -2 being the lowest and +2 the highest and best score. If you were to score all the lines, which is rarely the case, you could end up with a total score as low as -10 or as high as +10.

PRESENT:

Same explanations apply as in PAST with one extra line added for the in-laws, if applicable.

Therefore, the total score for this time dimension could be as low as -12, and as high as + 12.

FUTURE:

We once again have 5 lines. The total score will be between 0 and +10, since for the FUTURE, we can only expect or wish for the better, so there should be no negative scores.

0 means not applicable, +1 means some improvement, +2 means a substantial improvement.

The total score for the FUTURE will be the sum of the two subsections (add them together).

1. Family and Friends

- Health and trauma are not to be factored in. The only score that is graphed is that indicating "overall influence."

PAST	Health	Trauma	Not a total score but-→	Overall influence they have on you
	-1 to +1	-2 to 0		-2 to +2
Biological parents				
Siblings (Combine all siblings)				
Grandparents				
Adults other than biological parents				
Friends				
Total score -10 to +10				

PRESENT	Health	Trauma	Not a total score but-→	Overall influence they may have on you
	-1 to +1	-2 to 0		-2 to +2
Parents				
Siblings				
Grandparents				

Children				
In-Laws				
Friends				
Total score -12 to +12	Health	Trauma		Add together Health and Trauma scores
	0 to +1	0 to 1		0 to +2
"Parents"				
Siblings				
Children and/or adult children				
In-Laws				
Friends				
Total score 0 to +10				

Explanation of Dimension # 2 (Spouses and Ex-Spouses and/or Significant Others or Ex-Significant Others):

PAST:

For your past, you have the option to recall up to 3 people, including your current life partner if you were already involved together in the past.

There are at least 7 issues to consider, including alcohol and drug abuse, health, etc. For each of the 3 people, you write the OVERALL IMPRESSION of their influence on you at the end of the line, scoring them between -2 to +1. If you counted only ONE partner, the total overall impression will be between -2 to and +1. In case of 2 partners, the total overall impression will be between -4 and +2. For 3 partners, it will be between -6 and +3.

PRESENT:

The same possible 7 issues still apply but you will only score one current partner if you have one. The OVERALL IMPRESSION for that relationship could be anywhere from -3 if very poor up to +3 if very great. If there is no current relationship to score, write a 0.

FUTURE:

The same possible 7 issues still apply as you consider your wishes and expectations for improvement. If you do not wish to be involved in any relationship in the future, the score will be 0. If there are some negative issues currently, you can only wish for something better. Therefore the final score could be between 0 with +4 being the best case – no negative scores should be recorded for future goals.

2.   (Ex-SPOUSES AND Spouses And Ex-Significant Other and Ex-Significant Others

PAST	N/A	Alcohol/Drug abuse	Health issues	Family	Finances	As parents	Intimacy	Culture/ Religion	Overall impre-ssion
	0	-1 to 0	-1 to +1	-1 to +1	-1 to +1	-1 to +1	-1 to +1	-1 to +1	-2 to +1
# 1									
# 2									
# 3									

Up to the most significant 3

Total score -6 to +3

PRESENT	N/A	Alcohol/Drug abuse	Health issues	Family	Finances	As parents	Intimacy	Culture/ Religion	Overall impression
	0	-1 to 0	-2 to+2	-2 to +1	-2 to +2	-2 to +2	-2 to +2	-1 to +1	-3 to +3
Total score -3 to +3									

FUTURE	N/A	Alcohol/Drug abuse	Health issues	Family	Finances	As parents	Intimacy	Culture / Religion	Overall impress -ion
	0	0	-2 to +2	0 to +1	0 to +2	0 to +2	0 to +2	0 to +1	0 to +4
Total score 0 to +4									

Explanation of Dimension # 3: Living, Housing Conditions

PAST:

Compare your past living conditions to what you have in your current life, simply rank it between"painful" or "uncomfortable" and "comfortable." "Past" could be anytime you choose. It could be 5 or 10 years ago, in your childhood, adolescence, or adult life. The PAST score is either -2 ,-1, 0, or between 1 and 3. +3 is for very comfortable and is the very best score. You may want to write down which time period you are using for later comparisons.

PRESENT:

Score exactly the same way as for the PAST, between -2 (the worst) and +3 (the best) score.

FUTURE:

If you do not wish for any changes in your living conditions, your FUTURE score will be the same as for the PRESENT.

If there is room for improvement and the improvement would be significant, you could add 1 or even 2 points to the PRESENT score. If the wished-for improvement is very significant, you could add 3 points to the PRESENT score.

11

3. LIVING (HOUSING) CONDITIONS

PAST	Painful	Uncomfortable	Acceptable "So-So"	Comfortable	Score
					-2 to +3
How was your housing?	-2	-1	0	+1 to +3	
Total score -2 to +3					

PRESENT	Painful	Uncomfortable	Acceptable "So-So"	Comfortable	Score
					-2 to +3
How is your housing?	-2	-1	0	+1 to +3	
Total score -2 to +3					

FUTURE	Expected housing/living conditions in your future		Score
			0 to +6
	No change	Same score as present	
	Significant change	Same score as present + 1 or +2	
	Very significant change	Same score as present +3	
Total score 0 to +6			

Explanation of Dimension # 4: Health

PAST:

"Physical" refers to any major physical issue in your past. If you did poorly with it, the score could be -2 or -1. If you did very well with it, it could be +1 or +2. If you were physically healthy, give yourself a score of 1 or even 2.

A "major handicap" could be something as serious as blindness, paralysis, or any other significant impairment. If you did poorly with it, you give yourself a low score. If you did well with that major handicap, you deserve +1 or even +2. If you were lucky enough NOT to have any serious handicap in your past, you score yourself +2.

For "emotional or psychological issues," the same rationale as above applies, with your score varying between -2 and +2.

The total score is the addition of the 3 partial scores, and it will be between -6 and + 6.

PRESENT:

We still have the same 3 partial scores, and their sum will be your total score, between -6 and +6.

FUTURE:

This will score how you wish to deal with the same 3 issues in the future.

If you expect not to have any, your score will be +2 for each issue up to a maximum of +6. If there will realistically be some persistent issue(s) in your future, you score according to the improvement you expect to see. Therefore, it could be the same or better than in the PRESENT. The total score is between -6 and + 6, the same as for the PRESENT and the PAST. No one would wish or expect a worse condition than they currently have, so your FUTURE score should not be lower than the PRESENT.

4. HEALTH ISSUES

PAST	Physical	Major handicap	Emotional/ Psychological
	-2 to +2	-2 to +2	-2 to +2
Treated or Untreated			
Total score -6 to +6			

PRESENT	Physical	Major handicap	Emotional/ Psychological
	-2 to +2	-2 to +2	-2 to +2
Treated or Untreated			
Total score -6 to +6			

FUTURE	Physical	Major handicap	Emotional/ Psychological
	-2 to +2	-2 to +2	-2 to +2
Treated or Untreated			

Explanation of Dimension # 5: Education

If you ever received a grade school and/or a high school education, you cannot lose it. Therefore, it counts for the PAST, the PRESENT, and the FUTURE. That will be a score of 2 (1 + 1) for the PAST.

You will also add whatever education you have gained since then. For instance, 2 years of college would add another 1 point. You would then end up with a total score of 3 for the PRESENT.

In the FUTURE, you will add that goal to your future score. For instance, if you intend to attend 4 years of college, you add that to whatever you have scored in the PRESENT and the total would be +4.

EXAMPLE:

PAST:
Completion of either high school, or GED, or Special Education; Score is 1 +1.

PRESENT:
Completion of 2 years of college over the past few years, as opposed to the past years, you add another point. Total score is +3. If you happen to be currently enrolled in a school, trade school or college, give yourself a "credit" of +1 in overall score, even though you have not yet completed your current goal. The assumption is that you will finish.

FUTURE:
Let's say you're planning or wishing to return one day or to continue college and maybe get a total of 4 years of college. You would add another 1 point to what you have scored in the PRESENT and the total score will be 4.

The maximum total score of 6 means you went through many years of school, including trade school at one time and over 4 years of college

5. EDUCATION

	Incomplete	Complete	Score	PAST	PRESENT	FUTURE
	0	+1	0 to +1			
Grade school special education						
High school special education						
Trade school						
2 years college						
4 years college						
More than 4 years of college						
Total score 0 to +6						

Explanation of Dimension # 6: Finances

Whether you are single, married, or in a domestic relationship, as long as you're both contributing to the household income the scoring will be the same as if you were single.

PAST:

If your current age is 18 or younger, the score for PAST is not relevant and it should be 0. If your age is 19 or over, score the PAST using the following guidelines.

If the main source of your income came from your relatives, you score -1. If it was Government assistance, score 0. Your spouse +1 and other sources -1.

If you were not dependent on anyone but yourself, you have the option to score +1, + 2 or +3, according to how comfortable you felt financially.

The overall score for PAST will be whatever one score you feel comfortable with and will be between -1 and +3

PRESENT:

The same explanations are used as in PAST, with the final score being between -1 and + 3

FUTURE:

Here, you score your realistic expectations for the near or distant years to come (your choice).

If your main source of income will be from the government, such as Social Security or Disability benefits, the score could be 0 or +1.

If the main source of income is from a source other than the government, such as a retirement fund or a pension the score could be either +2 or +3.

If you remain mostly independent, then the score will be between 0 and + 3.

Do not add these numbers. The final score will be between 0 and 3.

6. FINANCES

PAST	Were you mainly dependent on...				Independent	Overall score
	-1	0	+1	-1	+1 to +3	-1 to +3
	Family	Government Assistance	Spouse	Other sources		
Total score -1 to +3						

PRESENT	Are you mainly dependent on...				Independent	Overall score
	-1	0	+1	-1	+1 to +3	-1 to +3
	Family	Government Assistance	Spouse	Other sources		
Total score -1 to +3						

19

FUTURE	Do you plan on being mainly dependent on...		Independent	Overall score
	0 to +1	+2 to +3	0 to +3	0 to +3
	Government Assistance	Other sources		
As a single person or As a couple				
Total score 0 to +3				

Explanation of Dimension # 7: Work Activities

PAST:

First line: If you never held a full-time job in the past due to a serious disability, your score should be either 0 or even +1 if it was still a positive experience. If you held one or more jobs in the PAST, keeping in mind the OVERALL job experience for the most significant jobs; the score can vary to -1 or 0 or +1.

Second line: Working as volunteer in the PAST is worth 0 or +1 to eventually be added to the first line score.

Third line: Having been a homemaker is worth 0 to +1, with +1 being a positive experience. That score will be added to the previous line(s).

Fourth line: If you were a student or served in the military service, you score 0 or +1. This will be added to the previous lines.

The total score for the PAST will be between -1 and + 4

PRESENT:

Use exactly the same explanations for the four lines as you did for the PAST. The total score will be between -1 and + 4.

FUTURE:

Some of us still plan to remain active after being officially retired, so there could be 2 partial scores. For example there may be one scoring for when you are 35, 55, or 70 and another scoring for when you quit holding a job.

First partial score: up to 4 lines to score, with a score between 0 and +4.

Second partial score: up to 3 lines, with a score between 0 and +3,

Therefore, the total score for the future could be between 0 and +7.

7. WORK ACTIVITIES

PAST	Disabled	Temporary	Permanent	Overall Impression
Most significant jobs: (-1 to +1) #1 #2 #3 #4				
Volunteering: (0 to +1)				
Homemaker: (0 to +1)				
Student/Military: (0 to +1)				
Total score -1 to +4				

PRESENT	Disabled	Temporary	Permanent	Overall Impression
Job: (-1 to +1)				
Volunteering: (0 to +1)				
Homemaker: (0 to +1)				
Student/Military: (0 to +1)				
Total score -1 to +4				

FUTURE	Disabled	Temporary	Permanent	Overall Impression
Before Retirement:				
Job: (0 to +1)				
Volunteering: (0 to +1)				
Homemaker: (0 to +1)				
Student/Military: (0 to +1)				
After Retirement:				
Volunteering: (0 to +1)				
Homemaker: (0 to +1)				
Student/Military: (0 to +1)				

Total score 0 to +7

Explanation of Dimension # 8: Chemical Dependency

There is no fixed definition about the amount of use, such as 'excessive' or
'moderate' use. Since this test means something only to you, try to be objective.
Don't be too lenient or too harsh on yourself – just be honest. It is up to each person
to decide whether to consider the use of marijuana as legal or illegal according to his
or her own convictions.

PAST:

Example: Years ago as an adult, you smoked moderately, perhaps less than a pack of cigarettes a day.
You would score -1. There was a time when you indulged in alcohol, yet not excessively or daily, You would
give yourself a score of -1. You were not abusing prescription meds, which is worth +1. You abused illegal
drugs on a steady basis, worth -2. Your total score is -3 for the PAST.

PRESENT:

Example: You quit smoking tobacco, which is worth +1. You still drink alcohol moderately, which is worth -1.
You now have a tendency to abuse prescription meds occasionally. This is another -1. You quit using any street drugs,

which is another +1. The total score for the PRESENT is 0.

FUTURE:

This score is for what you wish or expect in the years to come. Of course, the score can be the same or better than
the PRESENT but not worse.

Example: You remain tobacco free; score it +1. You still expect to do some light or moderate drinking, which
counts for a -1. You expect not to abuse medications or illegal drugs, each worth +1, thus another 2 points. Your total score is + 2 for the FUTURE.

8. CHEMICAL DEPENDENCY

Chemical	Duration (years)	Extent (estimate)	Score	PAST	PRESENT	FUTURE (expect ations)
				-8 to +4	-8 to +4	-4 to +4
Tobacco		None	+1			
		light or moderate	-1			
		variable	-1			
		excessive	-2			
Alcohol		none	+1			

		light or moderate	-1			
		variable	-1			
		excessive	-2			
Prescription Meds		none	+1			
		light or moderate	-1			
		variable	-1			
		excessive	-2			
Illegal drugs		none	+1			
		light or moderate	-1			
		variable	-1			
		excessive	-2			

Total score						

Explanation of Dimension # 9: Legal issues

PAST:

Unless you just turned 18 years of age, there are 2 lines to score. When you add those 2 lines, you may end up with a final PAST score between − 6 and +4.

Any illegal activity or incarceration in jail or prison is scored either -1 or -2. No illegal activity means +2.

The total PAST score for anyone over the age of 18 is between -6 and +4 when you add up the 2 lines. If you are 18 years of age or younger, the score will be between -3 and +2.

PRESENT:

For the PRESENT, only one line applies. The scoring is different than for the PAST.
No illegal activity now means a score of +4. In case of current (recent) illegal activity, the score could be either -1 or -2 and the total PRESENT score is between -3 and +4.

FUTURE:

Again, there is only one line. Since you are scoring your wishes or expectations, it can only be as good as, if not better than, the PRESENT score and the total score is between 0 and +4. There should be no score less than zero.

LEGAL ISSUES

PAST	DUI	DRUGS	JAIL	PRISON	Serious Crime	NONE	Score
	-1	-1	-1	-2 to -1	-2	+2	-3 to +2
Before 18 years old							
	-1	-1	-1	-2 to -1	-2	+2	-3 to +2
After 18 years old							
Total score -6 to +4							

PRESENT	DUI	DRUGS	JAIL	PRISON	Serious Crime	NONE	Score
Over the past year	-1	-1	-1	-2 to -1	-2	+4	-3 to +4
Total score -3 to +4							

FUTURE	DUI	DRUGS	JAIL	PRISON	Serious Crime	NONE	Score
						0 to +4	0 to +4
	0	0	0	0	0		
Total score 0 to +4							

Explanation of Dimension # 10: Sporting Activities, Arts, Education, Volunteering, Special talents

It is now time to score some activities that are less serious, yet often very significant in our lives.

There are the same 5 lines to score for all 3 different time dimensions - PAST, PRESENT and FUTURE--and you will score any that are applicable to your life. At the end of each line, you should end up with a score of 0 or +1 or +2, depending on the quality of your involvement in that activity. Your total score is the sum total of the scores obtained on the 5 lines. It could be as low as 0 or as high as 10 for each time dimension.

Sporting activities: Any physical activity practiced on a regular basis which is done primarily for promoting good health. Examples include jogging, yoga, aerobics, or hiking

Arts: Playing or writing music, painting, arts and crafts

Education: Cultural or educational activity practiced mostly for self-gratifying purposes (not necessarily for the purpose of getting a degree)

Volunteering: Giving of your time, attention or devotion on a regular basis, be it part-time or even full-time

Special talents: Being especially gifted in athletic or artistic activities, such as choir singing, painting, writing, swimming, javelin throwing

PAST and PRESENT: The total score for each of these will be between 0 and +10

As always, the FUTURE reflects what we wish, plan, or project in the best circumstances. Your total score could be much higher than in PAST or PRESENT - depending of the extent of your dreams.

10. *SPORTING ACTIVITIES, ARTS, EDUCATION, VOLUNTEERING, SPECIAL TALENTS*

PAST	none	Minimal	Optimal	Score
	0	1	2	0 to +2
Sporting Activities				
Arts				
Education				
Volunteering				
Special Talents				
Total score 0 to +10				

PRESENT	none	Minimal	Optimal	Score
	0	1	2	0 to +2
Sporting Activities				
Arts				
Education				
Volunteering				
Special Talents				
Total score 0 to +10				

FUTURE	none	Minimal	Optimal	Score
	0	1	2	0 to +2
Sporting Activities				
Arts				
Education				
Volunteering				
Special Talents				
Total score 0 to +10				

Explanation of Dimension # 11: Cultural and/or Ethnicity Issues

PAST:
Here you will score your past racial, religious, or cultural experiences. If there was any significant conflict in any or
all of those areas, such as while being raised by your parents, having adopted parents, parents of mixed ethnic or religious backgrounds, or sharing part of your past life in a conflicted interracial relationship, then your score is -2. If there were no conflicts, the score is +2. In a best-case scenario, the PAST experiences were very positive and your score is + 4. Your past score could be -2, +2 or +4.

PRESENT:
Use the same guidelines as in PAST with a final score between -2 and +4.

FUTURE:
You will score here the improvements (if any) that you can expect to see in the years to come. The score could be as good or even better than the PRESENT. The final score will be between -1 and +4.

11. CULTURAL AND/OR ETHNIC ISSUES

PAST	Conflict	No conflict	Optimal	Score
	-2	+2	+4	-2 to +4
Past Racial/Religious/Cultural Experiences...				
Total score -2 to +4				

PRESENT	Conflict	No conflict	Optimal	Score
	-2	+2	+4	-2 to +4
Present Racial/Religious/Cultural Experiences...				
Total score -2 to +4				

FUTURE	Conflict	No conflict	Optimal	Score
	-1	+2	+4	-1 to +4
Rate your future Racial/Religious/Cultural Expectations...				
Total score -1 to +4				

33

Explanation of Dimension # 12: Religion

PAST:

Exposure and commitment to any religious activities or practice may be experienced very differently from one individual to another. There will be 2 scores to add together:

First line: Were you forced in the PAST (at any age) to be involved? If so, you score -1. If there was NO exposure to any consistent religious experience, the score would be 0. If the exposure was minimal or not consistent, the score could be 0 or even + 1. If you really felt a commitment to your religious beliefs, you would score +2

Second line: This will be another partial score.

If the overall experience in the PAST left you with a negative impression, the score is -1. If that experience was mostly neutral, the score is 0. If that experience was positive one, you could give it a score of +1, +2 or even +3. Now you add the 2 scores from lines 1 and 2 to get a total score between -2 and +5.

PRESENT:

Score the same way as PAST to reach a total score between -2 and +5.

FUTURE:

You have the choices between the following:

If you expect the same as is the PRESENT, the score should be between -2 and +5. Neutral means no wish or need to be involved in any religious experience. Your score could be either 0 or +1. If you wish more involvement or commitment than you currently have, the score will be between +1 and +5.

12. RELIGION

PAST	Forced	None	Minimal or Variable	Committed	Score
Any age	-1	0	0 to +1	+2	-1 to +2

Overall experience	Negative			-1	
	Neutral			0	
	Positive			+1 to +3	
Total score -2 to +5					

PRESENT	Forced	None	Minimal or Variable	Committed	Score
	-1	0	0 to +1	+2	-1 to +2

Overall experience	Negative			-1	
	Neutral			0	
	Positive			+1 to +3	
Total score -2 to +5					

FUTURE	Same as present	Neutral	Improved
	-2 to +5	0 to +1	+1 to +5
Total score -2 to +5			

Explanation of Dimension # 13: Political Issues: Conflicts, Involvements and Interest in Politics

PAST:

In this area of political issues, matters, and involvements, if you experienced conflicts with others, such as relatives, a spouse, close friends or even at work, then your score will be -1.

If there was an absence of political activities or interests, your score is +1.

If you had minimal, yet existent, political activities or interests, your score is 0.

In the case of optimal, gratifying political involvement, your score is +4.

Your final score is between -1 and +4.

PRESENT:

Use the same guidelines as in PAST and your score will be between -1 and +4.

FUTURE: You, of course, do not wish or expect any conflict in this area in the future. Therefore the score of -1 is NOT available. The final score will be +1 in case of no involvement wished in the future , 0 for a minimal involvement, and +4 for an optimal involvement in political issues or matters.

13. POLITICAL ISSUES

PAST	Conflict with significant others	Minimal	None	Optimal	Score
	-1	0	+1	+4	-1 to +4
Were you involved in politics?					
Total score -1 to +4					

PRESENT	Conflict with significant others	Minimal	None	Optimal	Score
	-1	0	+1	+4	-1 to +4
Are you involved in politics?					
Total score -1 to +4					

FUTURE	Minimal	None	Optimal	Score
	0	+1	+4	0 to +4
Will you be involved in politics?				
Total score 0 to +4				

Explanation of Dimension #14 (if applicable): Military

This last dimension pertains only to those of us who served, are still serving, or who will serve in the Military in any country. It applies to any of the branch of the Military as well as the National Guard, be it as active duty or reservist. If this does not apply to you, you can skip this dimension. For this dimension there are 2 partial scores in the 3 time dimensions which you will add together for a final score.

PAST:
First partial score. For one term, whether completed or not, a neutral experience would score 0, a positive one would score +1. If you renewed for one or more terms, you score +2. If you served as a career person you will score the highest, +3. Your first partial score could be between 0 and +3.

Second partial score: This deals with the kind of discharge you received. (If you are still serving, score yourself based on what you reasonably expect to receive). If dishonorable, the score is -2, if other than honorable, the score is -1, general is +1 and if honorable, +2.

You then add those 2 partial scores and the total PAST score will be as low as -2 or as high as +5.

PRESENT:
If you are not currently involved in the service, you will use the same score as you did in the PAST, for a total between -2 and +5. If you are currently involved in the military, you score separately the 2 partial scores based on your current situation and add them to get a final score between -2 and +5.

FUTURE:

Once again you will add 2 partial scores. If you are planning to be involved in the Service in the future, your total score will be between 0 and +5. Negative scores are not allowed because nobody would wish or plan for a negative discharge. If you are NOT planning any further involvement, the total score will be whatever you achieved in the PRESENT.

#14: MILITARY	Score	PAST	PRESENT	FUTURE
Not applicable	0			
One term not completed or completed	0 to +1			
Renewed completed term	+2			
Career	+3			
# 1 Partial score	0 to +3			
Discharge type				
Dishonorable	-2			
Others than honorable	-1			
General	+1			
Honorable	+2			
# 2 Partial score	-2 to +2			
Total score		-2 to +5	-2 to +5	0 to +5

Proper Sequence for the 13 or 14 Dimensions and Score Ranges

	Dimensions	PAST	PRESENT	FUTURE
# 1	Family and friends	-10 to +10	-12 to +12	0 to +10
# 2	(Ex) Spouses and/or (ex) Significant Others	-6 to +3	-3 to +3	0 to +4
# 3	Living (Housing) Conditions	-2 to +3	-2 to +3	0 to +6
# 4	Health issues	-6 to +6	-6 to +6	-6 to +6
# 5	Education	0 to +6	0 to +6	0 to +6
# 6	Finances	-1 to +3	-1 to +3	0 to +3
# 7	Work Activities	-1 to +4	-1 to +4	0 to +7
# 8	Chemical dependency	-8 to +4	-8 to +4	-4 to +4
# 9	Legal issues	-6 to +4	-3 to +4	0 to +4
# 10	Sporting activities, Arts, Education, Volunteering, and Special talents	0 to +10	0 to +10	0 to +10
# 11	Cultural, Ethnical issues	-2 to +4	-2 to +4	-1 to +4
# 12	Religious issues	-2 to +5	-2 to +5	-2 to +5
# 13	Political issues	-1 to +4	-1 to +4	0 to +4
# 14	Military issues	-2 to +5	-2 to +5	0 to +5

	PAST	PRESENT	FUTURE
Score total range for 13 dimensions	-45 to +66	-41 to +65	-13 to +73
Score total range for 14 dimensions	-47 to +71	-43 to +70	-13 to +78

41

My total scoring – SAMPLE SCORES

Dimen-sions	Date : 1-1-2014			Date :			Date :			Date :		
	Past	Present	Future	Past	Present	Future	Past	Present	Future	Past	Present	Future
#1	-2	-9	+5									
#2	-3	+1	+3									
#3	-1	-2	+4									
#4	-4	-5	+1									
#5	+1	+2	+2									
#6	+0	+1	+2									
#7	-1	+1	+3									
#8	-4	-3	-2									
#9	-5	-2	+2									
#10	+1	+1	+3									
#11	-1	-1	+4									
#12	-2	+0	+5									
#13	+0	+0	+4									
#14	-1	+1	+4									
Total	-22	-17	+40									

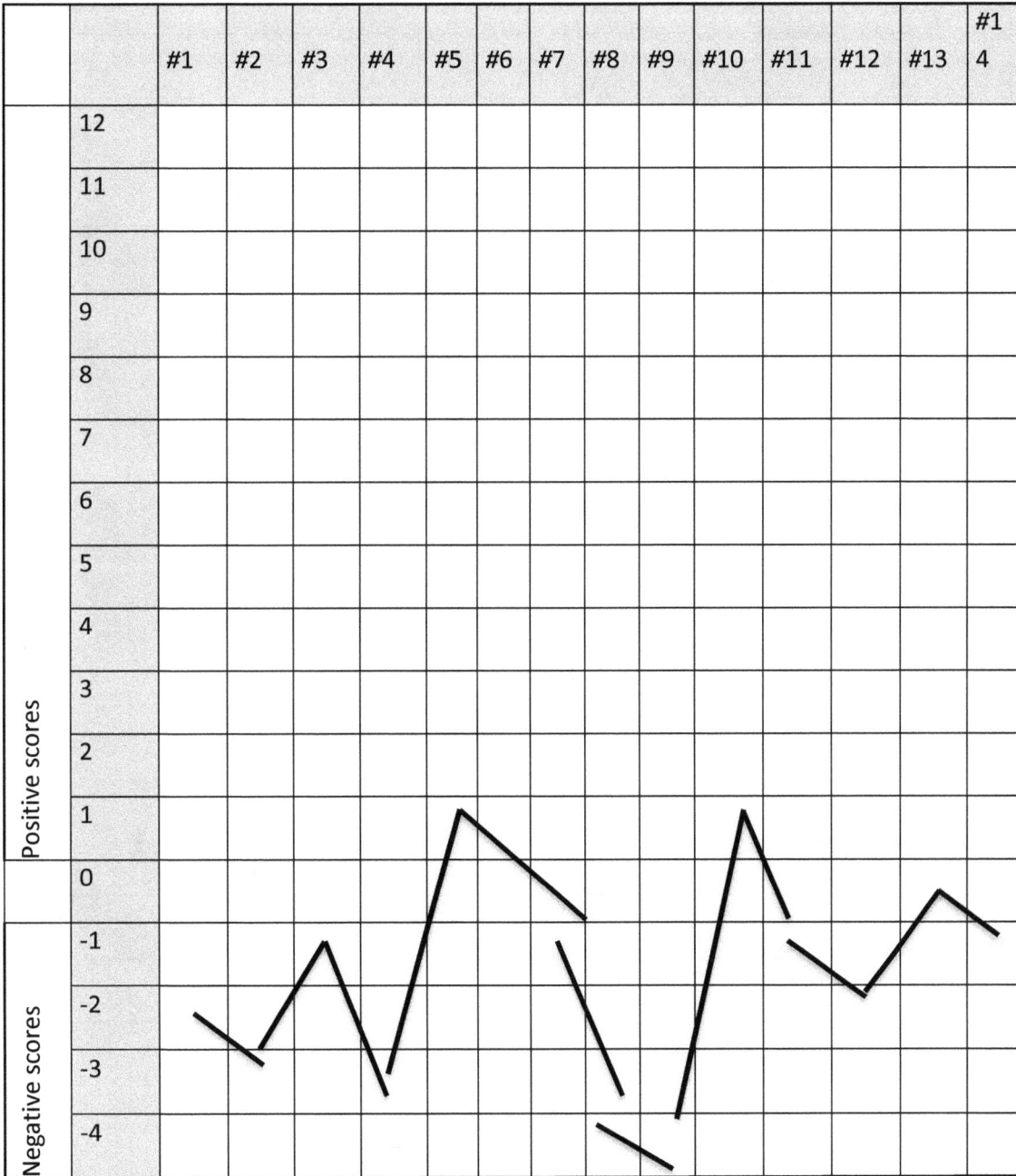

**BEGIN
G1**   PAST GRAPH: SAMPLE SCORES

Scoring date :

		#1	#2	#3	#4	#5	#6	#7	#8	#9	#10	#11	#12	#13	#14
Positive scores	12														
	11														
	10														
	9														
	8														
	7														
	6														
	5														
	4														
	3														
	2														
	1														
	0														
Negative scores	-1														
	-2														
	-3														
	-4														

43

	-5														
	-6														
	-7														
	-8														
	-9														
	-10														
	-11														
	-12														

END G1

BEGIN G2

PRESENT GRAPH: SAMPLE SCORES

Scoring date :

		#1	#2	#3	#4	#5	#6	#7	#8	#9	#10	#11	#12	#13	#14
	12														
	11														
Positive scores	10														
	9														
	8														

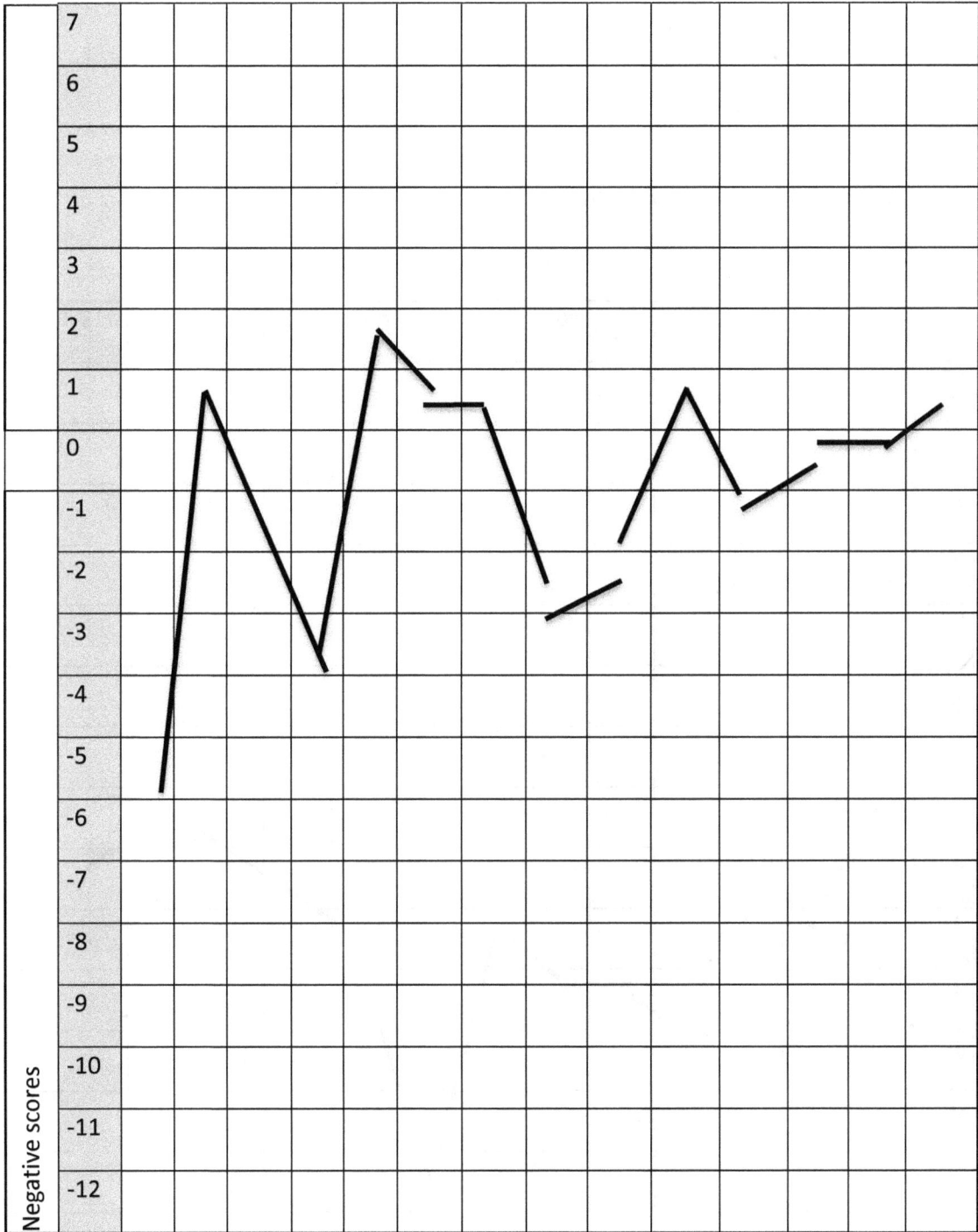

	7															
	6															
	5															
	4															
	3															
	2															
	1															
	0															
	-1															
	-2															
	-3															
	-4															
	-5															
	-6															
	-7															
	-8															
	-9															
	-10															
	-11															
Negative scores	-12															

END G2

45

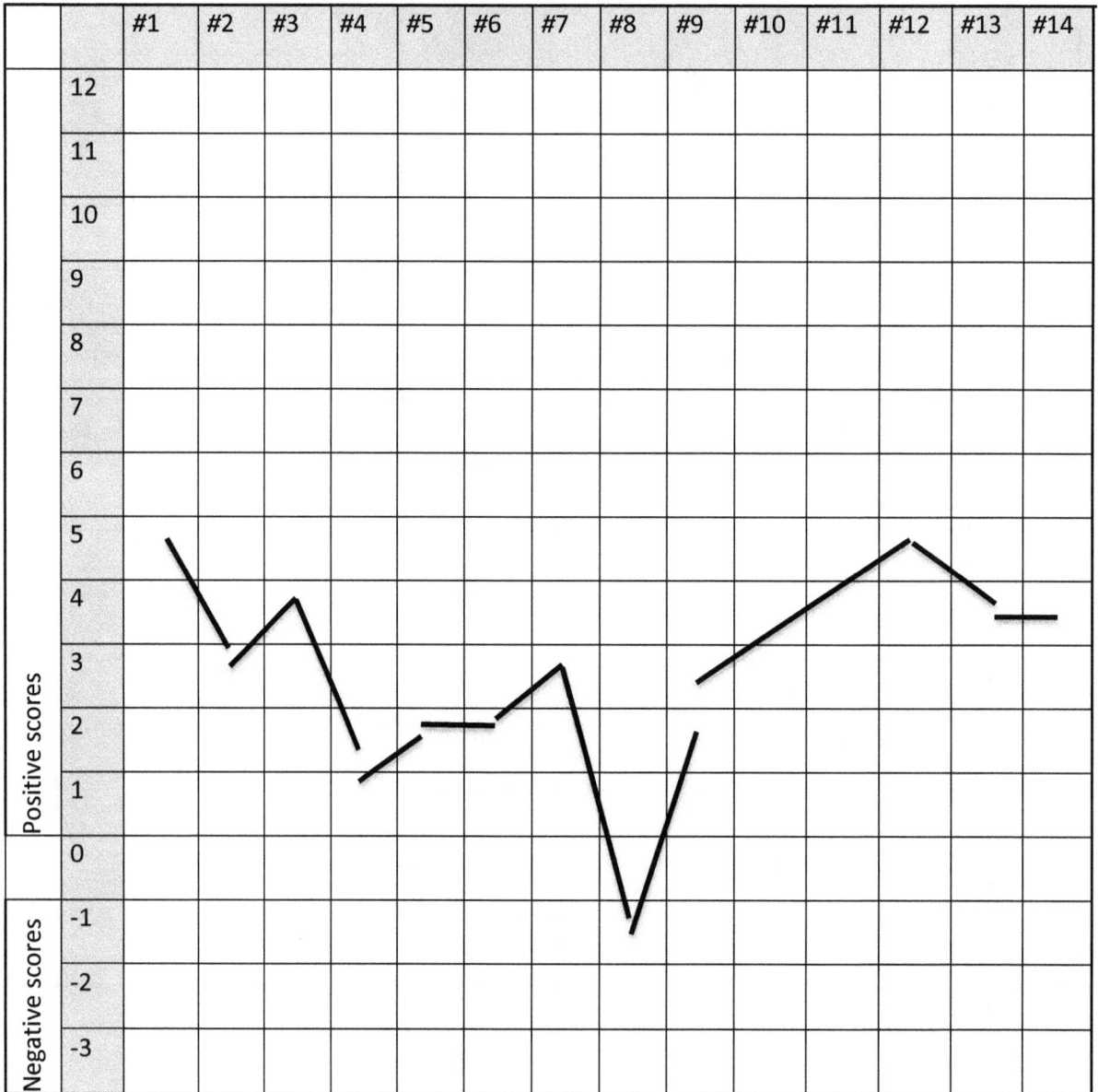

BEGIN G3

FUTURE GRAPH: SAMPLE SCORES

Scoring date :

		#1	#2	#3	#4	#5	#6	#7	#8	#9	#10	#11	#12	#13	#14
Positive scores	12														
	11														
	10														
	9														
	8														
	7														
	6														
	5														
	4														
	3														
	2														
	1														
	0														
Negative scores	-1														
	-2														
	-3														

-4														
-5														
-6														
-7														
-8														
-9														
-10														
-11														
-12														

END G3

BEGIN G4

PAST GRAPH: FULL RANGE of SCORES

Scoring date :

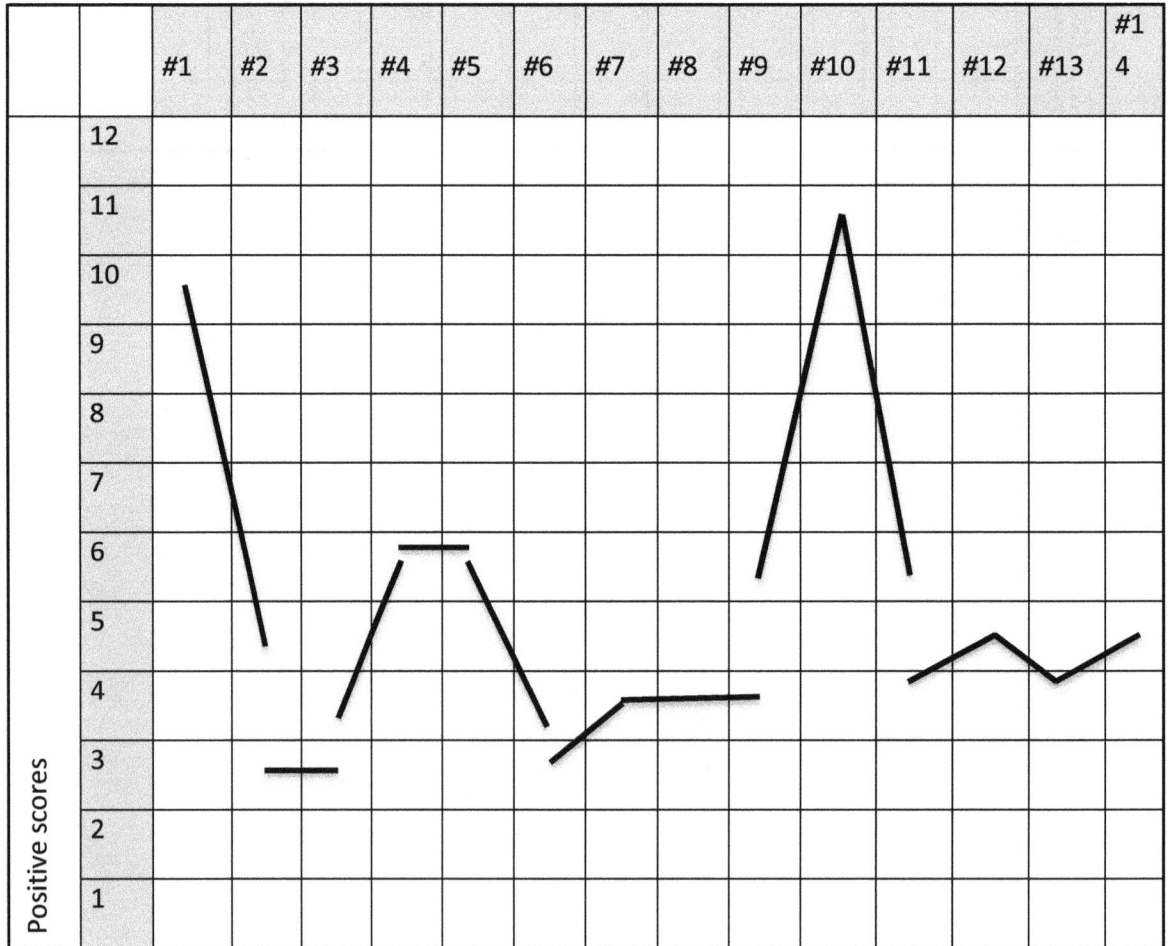

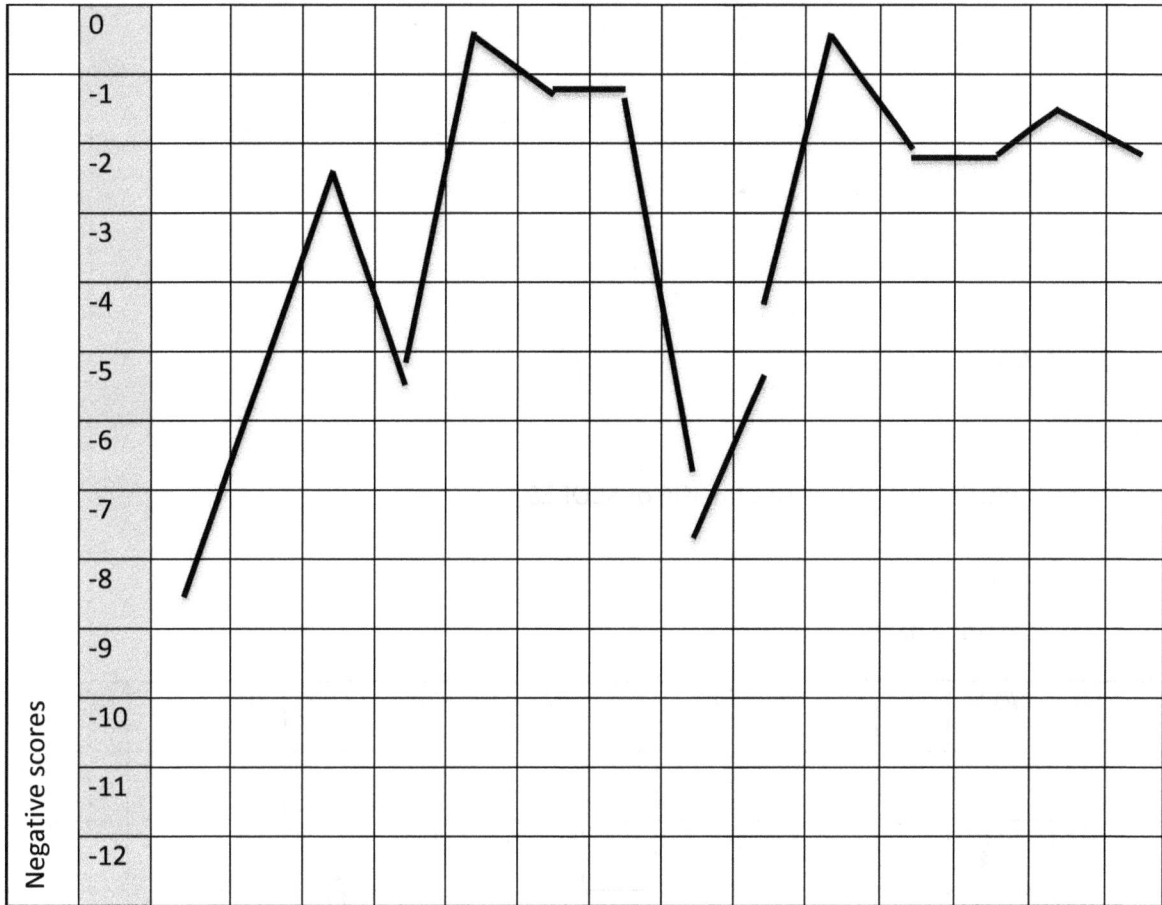

END G4

BEGIN G5

PRESENT GRAPH: FULL RANGE of SCORES

Scoring date :

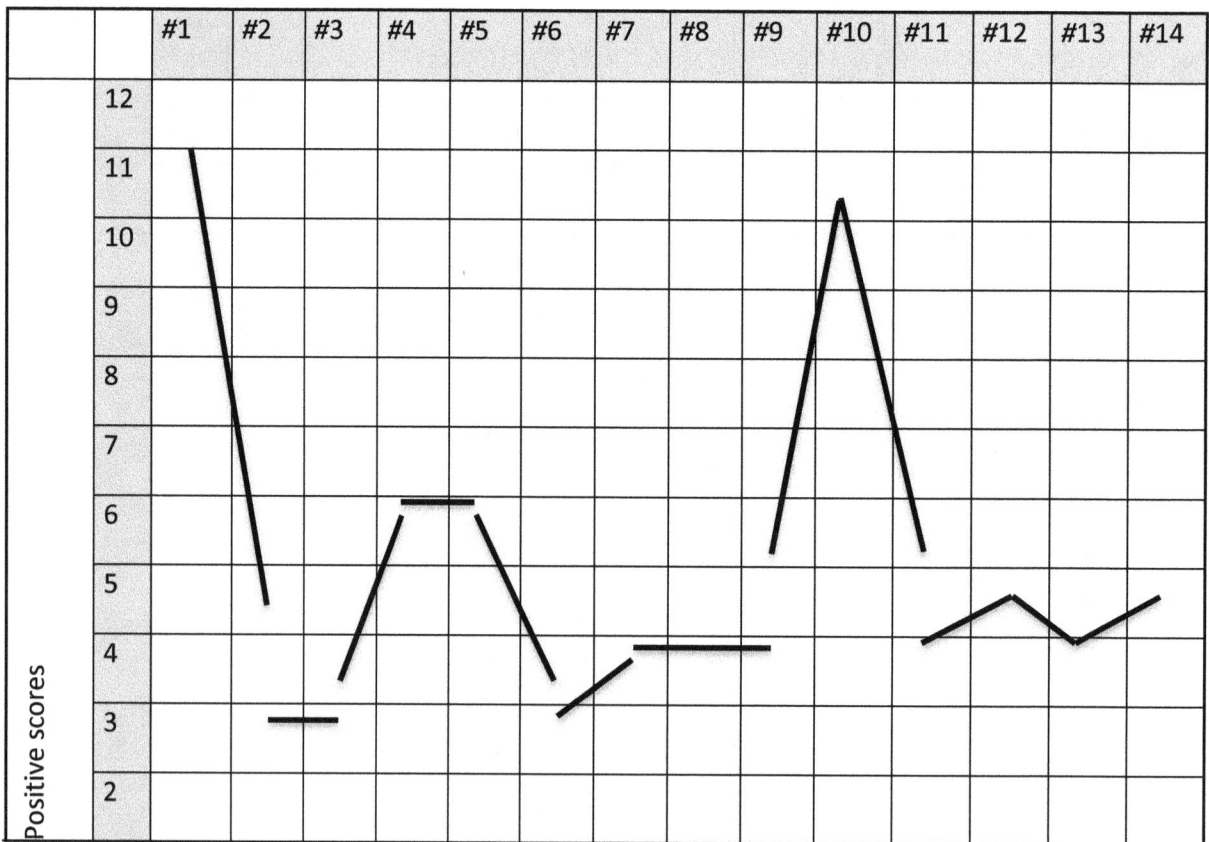

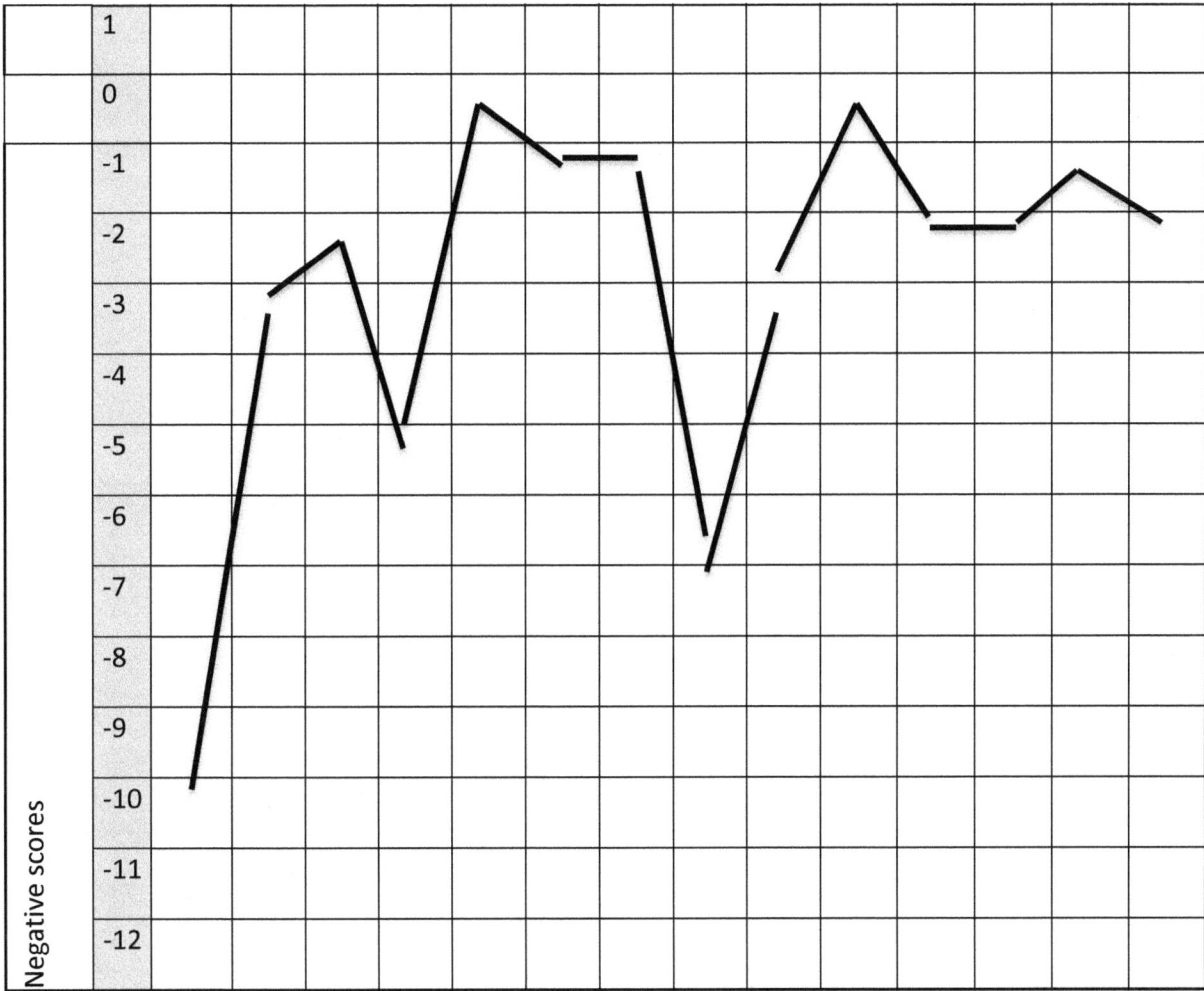

END G5

51

BEGIN G6

FUTURE GRAPH: FULL RANGE of SCORES

Scoring date :

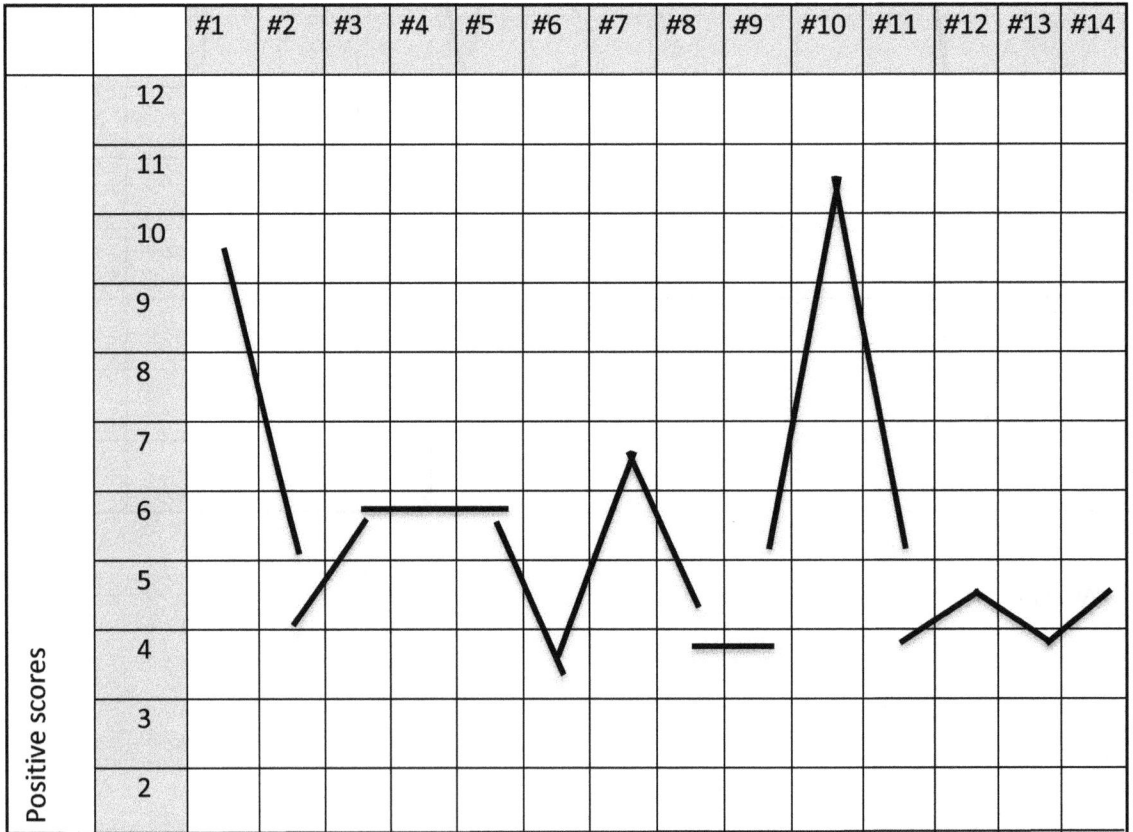

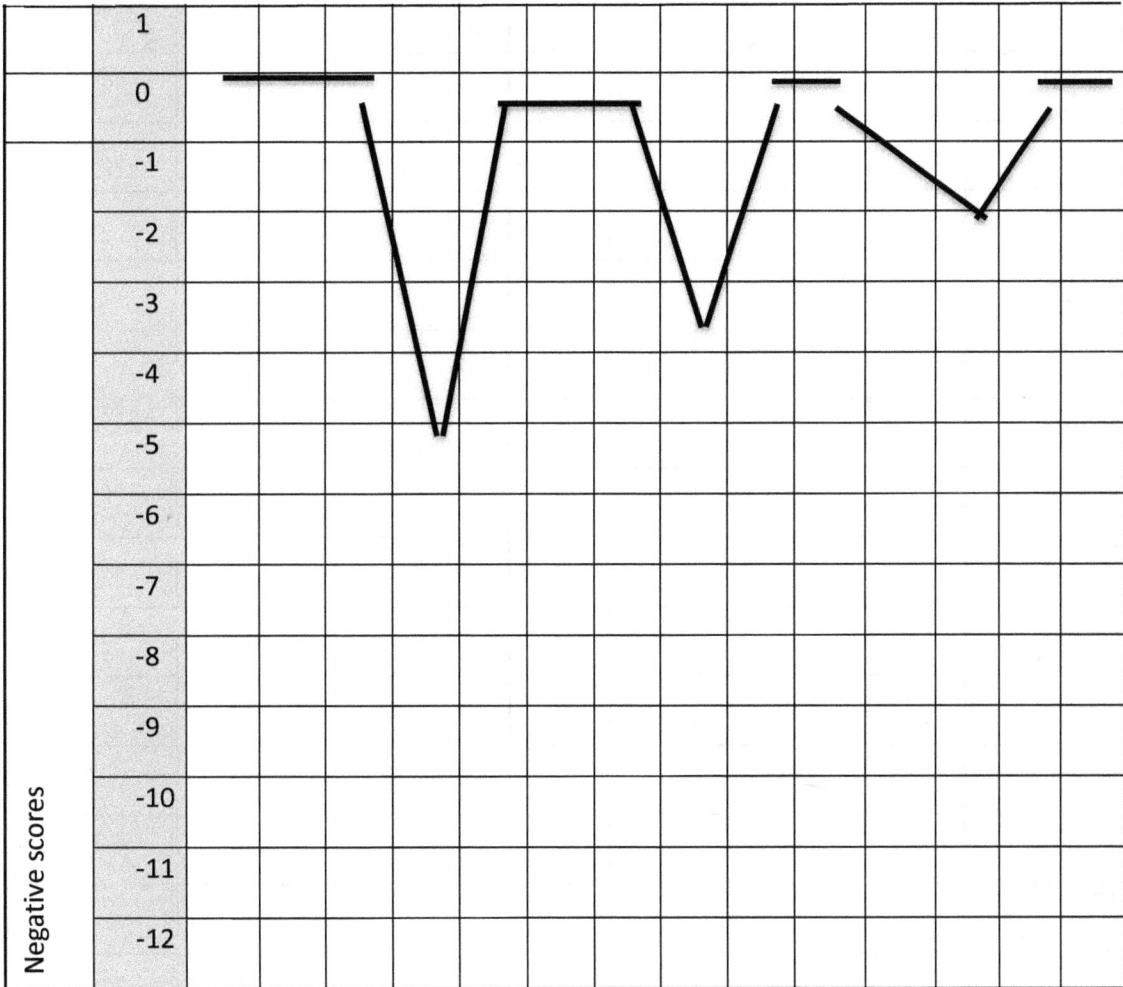

END G6

My total scoring

	Date :			Date :			Date :			Date :		
	Past	Present	Future	Past	Present	Future	Past	Present	Future	Past	Present	Future
#1												
#2												
#3												
#4												
#5												
#6												
#7												
#8												
#9												
#10												
#11												
#12												
#13												
#14												
Total												

54

My total scoring

	Date :			Date :			Date :			Date :		
	Past	Present	Future	Past	Present	Future	Past	Present	Future	Past	Present	Future
#1												
#2												
#3												
#4												
#5												
#6												
#7												
#8												
#9												
#10												
#11												
#12												
#13												
#14												
Total												

My total scoring

	Date :			Date :			Date :			Date :		
	Past	Present	Future	Past	Present	Future	Past	Present	Future	Past	Present	Future
#1												
#2												
#3												
#4												
#5												
#6												
#7												
#8												
#9												
#10												
#11												
#12												
#13												
#14												
Total												

My total scoring

	Date :			Date :			Date :			Date :		
	Past	Present	Future	Past	Present	Future	Past	Present	Future	Past	Present	Future
#1												
#2												
#3												
#4												
#5												
#6												
#7												
#8												
#9												
#10												
#11												
#12												
#13												
#14												
Total												

BEGIN G7

My PAST: Scoring Graph

Scoring date :

Positive scores		#1	#2	#3	#4	#5	#6	#7	#8	#9	#10	#11	#12	#13	#14
	12														
	11														
	10														
	9														
	8														
	7														
	6														
	5														
	4														
	3														
	2														
	1														

	0													
	-1													
	-2													
	-3													
	-4													
	-5													
	-6													
	-7													
	-8													
	-9													
Negative scores	-10													
	-11													
	-12													

END G7

59

BEGIN G8

My PAST: Scoring Graph

Scoring date :

		#1	#2	#3	#4	#5	#6	#7	#8	#9	#10	#11	#12	#13	#14
	12														
	11														
	10														
	9														
	8														
	7														
	6														
	5														
	4														
Positive scores	3														
	2														
	1														

	0												
	-1												
	-2												
	-3												
	-4												
	-5												
	-6												
	-7												
	-8												
	-9												
Negative scores	-10												
	-11												
	-12												

END G8

61

BEGIN G9

My PAST: Scoring Graph

Scoring date :

		#1	#2	#3	#4	#5	#6	#7	#8	#9	#10	#11	#12	#13	#14
	12														
	11														
	10														
	9														
	8														
	7														
	6														
	5														
	4														
Positive scores	3														
	2														
	1														

	0													
	-1													
	-2													
	-3													
	-4													
	-5													
	-6													
	-7													
	-8													
	-9													
Negative scores	-10													
	-11													
	-12													

END G9

BEGIN G10

My PAST: Scoring Graph

Scoring date :

		#1	#2	#3	#4	#5	#6	#7	#8	#9	#10	#11	#12	#13	#14
	12														
	11														
	10														
	9														
	8														
	7														
	6														
	5														
	4														
Positive scores	3														
	2														
	1														

	0												
Negative scores	-1												
	-2												
	-3												
	-4												
	-5												
	-6												
	-7												
	-8												
	-9												
	-10												
	-11												
	-12												

END G10

BEGIN G11

My PRESENT: Scoring Graph

Scoring date :

Positive scores		#1	#2	#3	#4	#5	#6	#7	#8	#9	#10	#11	#12	#13	#14
	12														
	11														
	10														
	9														
	8														
	7														
	6														
	5														
	4														
	3														
	2														
	1														

66

	0													
	-1													
	-2													
	-3													
	-4													
	-5													
	-6													
	-7													
	-8													
	-9													
Negative scores	-10													
	-11													
	-12													

END G11

67

BEGIN G12

My PRESENT: Scoring Graph

Scoring date :

		#1	#2	#3	#4	#5	#6	#7	#8	#9	#10	#11	#12	#13	#14
	12														
	11														
	10														
	9														
	8														
	7														
	6														
	5														
Positive scores	4														
	3														
	2														
	0														

	-1														
	-2														
	-3														
	-4														
	-5														
	-6														
	-7														
	-8														
	-9														
Negative scores	-10														
	-11														
	-12														

END G12

BEGIN G13

My PRESENT: Scoring Graph

Scoring date :

		#1	#2	#3	#4	#5	#6	#7	#8	#9	#10	#11	#12	#13	#14
	12														
	11														
Positive scores	10														
	9														

69

8														
7														
6														
5														
4														
3														
2														
1														
0														
-1														
-2														
-3														
-4														
-5														
-6														
-7														
-8														
-9														
-10														
-11														
-12														

Negative scores

END G13

BEGIN G14

My PRESENT: Scoring Graph

Scoring date :

		#1	#2	#3	#4	#5	#6	#7	#8	#9	#10	#11	#12	#13	#14
	12														
	11														
	10														
	9														
	8														
	7														
	6														
	5														
	4														
Positive scores	3														
	2														
	1														

	0														
	-1														
	-2														
	-3														
	-4														
	-5														
	-6														
	-7														
	-8														
	-9														
Negative scores	-10														
	-11														
	-12														

END G14

BEGIN G15

My FUTURE: Scoring Graph

Scoring date :

		#1	#2	#3	#4	#5	#6	#7	#8	#9	#10	#11	#12	#13	#14
	12														
	11														
	10														
	9														
	8														
	7														
	6														
	5														
	4														
Positive scores	3														
	2														
	1														

73

0															
-1															
-2															
-3															
-4															
-5															
-6															
-7															
-8															
-9															
-10															
-11															
-12															

Negative scores

END G15

BEGIN G16

My FUTURE: Scoring Graph

Scoring date :

		#1	#2	#3	#4	Evaluation of dimension #	#6	#7	#8	#9	#10	#11	#12	#13	#14
	12														
	11														
	10														
	9														
	8														
	7														
	6														
	5														
	4														
Positive scores	3														
	2														
	1														

	0														
Negative scores	-1														
	-2														
	-3														
	-4														
	-5														
	-6														
	-7														
	-8														
	-9														
	-10														
	-11														
	-12														

END G16

76

BEGIN G17

My FUTURE: Scoring Graph

Scoring date :

		#1	#2	#3	#4	#5	#6	#7	#8	#9	#10	#11	#12	#13	#14
	12														
	11														
	10														
	9														
	8														
	7														
	6														
	5														
	4														
Positive scores	3														
	2														
	1														

0															
-1															
-2															
-3															
-4															
-5															
-6															
-7															
-8															
-9															
-10															
-11															
-12															

Negative scores

END G17

My FUTURE: Scoring Graph

Scoring date :

Positive scores		#1	#2	#3	#4	#5	#6	#7	#8	#9	#10	#11	#12	#13	#14
	12														
	11														
	10														
	9														
	8														
	7														
	6														
	5														
	4														
	3														
	2														
	1														

	0														
	-1														
	-2														
	-3														
	-4														
	-5														
	-6														
	-7														
	-8														
	-9														
Negative scores	-10														
	-11														
	-12														

END G18

Part Two
Aristotle Modernized:
Constituent Elements of Health
and Happiness
£

"Do something wonderful.

People may imitate it."

- Albert Schweitzer

Premises

Aristotle, the great Greek thinker and philosopher, postulated that the one single thing that all people seek throughout their lives is happiness. Modern philosophers may argue with that assertion, but Aristotle based his position on carefully studying the actual behavior of people. He would feel that if we all took the time to observe the way he did, there would be sufficient confirmation of his position and beliefs.

This interactive study program works on the assumption that Aristotle's claim is essentially correct. All of us ultimately want to be happy. Of course, the degree of happiness each person may obtain is also influenced by many variables that may be beyond our control. Good physical or mental health may be partially attributed to good genetics, and genes vary greatly from one individual to another. Social status or the ability to garner financial or other resources can also be influenced by factors outside of one's control. Even the capacity for learning is subject to outside influences including genetics, childhood nutrition, availability of appropriate education and other factors.

Of course, many people seek out the wrong things in their pursuit to find personal happiness. These may include street drugs, abuse or misuse of prescription medications or even over-the-counter remedies, excessive use of alcohol, extreme indulgence in food, pursuit of unhealthy relationships, greed or excessive need for material things, or any number of other poor coping mechanisms. These self-ordered "happiness solutions" are initially thought to bring feelings of wellness or happiness but usually lead one down a path of misery or even death.

The pursuit of happiness brings back memories of two very different patients. The first man asked me during our first therapeutic encounter to write him a check for one million dollars. He said that this would bring him happiness. Another patient was a woman who lived in impoverished conditions and yet was able to save up a few thousand dollars over the course of several years in order to make a donation to the local Humane Society when she passed away. This was her very special road to achieve happiness.

Almost everyone can improve their measure of happiness and drag themselves from the abyss of misery and despair. This book will give you some of the appropriate steps outlined in this interactive program. However, there is one note of caution for anyone who undertakes this journey. It is important to understand the popular saying that admonishes us to recognize and to accept the things we cannot change, to summon the courage to change the things that we can, and to develop the wisdom to know the difference. There will always be some things about one's self or one's life that we can neither control nor improve. There are, however, many things that we can change in a positive fashion. The key to this solution is to believe that change is possible and to know what we are capable of achieving.

This interactive guide embodies a number of the principles covered in Aristotle's treatise on happiness. In some ways, this study is more comprehensive than Aristotle's because it is more interactive, self-driven, and is more in-line with modern medical and psychological approaches to happiness. This guide allows the participant to react, interact or respond to the materials in ways that are designed to help clarify thinking and set more realistic personal goals.

Rating Yourself

In the next few sections, you will be asked and prompted to identify your potentials, strengths and weaknesses. You will be asked to read questions, think about them, and decide on an honest self-rating that reflects your thoughts on various aspects of wellness. You will also be asked to provide an explanation as to why you rated yourself as you did. These ratings will help you to identify your strong points and your liabilities. Doing this should help to give you a clearer idea as to the measure of happiness you have enjoyed at a given time in your life. This tool will also help you become more in touch with the areas of your life that are most in need of improvement.

Here is how the system works. At the beginning of each subcategory, you are given a line where you will enter your personal rating. Your choices range from -10 to +10 with -10 being the worst it could be and +10 being the best possible rating. A zero indicates that you are not sure or you feel that you are completely neutral. The lower the negative rating, the more likely you are to remind yourself that improvement is needed in this particular area. Conversely, the higher the positive rating, the more likely you are to understand that you can focus your attention on other areas that are more in need of improvement. Remember, a zero rating means that you are not sure. These are the ratings that will be most interesting to continue to watch and make efforts to move into the positive ranges.

Below the line for recording your ratings are some prompt questions that will help you decide what your personal score should be. This is then followed by some blank lines for you to list the reasons for the score that you gave yourself. This will be helpful when you come back to these scores later for review or contemplation. The explanations will help you remember what details you were considering when rating yourself a particular way.

So what do these average scores tell us? This number will give you a visual representation of where you are TODAY in each of these categories. A score of +10 means everything is wonderful. A score of -10 means you have a lot to work on in this category to achieve happiness and a sense of fulfillment.

The goal of any self-help tool such as this is not only to show you where you are now but also to give you an idea of where you want to be in the future. This tool can be used time and time again. Come back to this assessment in the future when you have implemented some strategies to help improve your life, and you will see how your scores change over time. Some may be higher and some may be lower as priorities change over time.

There are no right answers or wrong answers. There are also no 'magic' tools to suddenly make your life better. This being said, by knowing where you are and where you would like to be, you will be better prepared to make changes in the right direction.

SET NUMBER ONE

Principle I

Physical, Mental, Emotional and Spiritual Wellness

The better and more complete your physical, mental, emotional and spiritual health becomes, the greater the measure of happiness you will achieve in life. When our lives are plagued by chronic illnesses, and aches and pains, or if we happen to be constantly vulnerable to the common cold or other ailments, our morale deteriorates and so does our delight in life.

Being constantly out of sorts is often the result of some physical problems that can easily be remedied. The worst thing to do is to do nothing. The first thing we ought to do is to get a proper medical diagnosis. If nothing can be done to relieve a medical issue, then our task is to learn to accept that which cannot be changed, to adapt to some limitations of our activity level, and eventually compensate for those limitations in other areas of our lives.

One example of this kind of compensation and adaptation is illustrated by the famous impressionist painter, Renoir. In his last 25 years of his active artistic life, he suffered from debilitating arthritis. His passion for painting, including 400 hundred masterpieces in his last 10 years, did not subside with his physical limitations. Instead, he tied his brushes to his hands and arms since he was unable to hold them tightly. He also found and developed sophisticated ways to access his easels.

Another much younger artist became extremely depressed all the way to the point of considering suicide. He had found out that his severe retinal deterioration was going to prevent him from finishing 25 paintings that he was scheduled to show in a local art gallery. Therapeutic intervention helped him to realize that he could still enjoy a few more months of his artistic creativity rather than focus on the quantity of paintings he could produce.

Yet another example of this phenomenon was demonstrated by a personal patient of mine. He was a very bright man in his mid-fifties, but he was becoming very depressed as he realized he could no longer run his normal five miles every morning. Through some short term individual therapy, he was able to accept the fact that some physiological changes had gradually occurred. He also discovered that 2 miles of daily jogging could be just as enjoyable and with a lot less pain. He had the option to lament and get more depressed, but instead he refused to give in to his gradually worsening limitations.

Following the instructions provided in the last section, it is time to rate yourself on the following elements that affect your general wellness.

A. Physical Health

1) Diet

-10 -9 -8 -7 -6 -5 -4 -3 -2 -1 0 +1 +2 +3 +4 +5 +6
+7 +8 +9 +10

Do you eat a balanced diet? How often do you indulge in "junk food"? Does your diet include fruits? Green vegetables? Excessive amounts of meat? Do you use excessive amounts of caffeine? Artificial sweeteners? Tobacco? Appetite suppressants?

Why did you rate yourself the way you did about your diet?

_____
_____

_____
_____

_____
_____

2) Weight control

_____

-10 -9 -8 -7 -6 -5 -4 -3 -2 -1 0 +1 +2 +3 +4 +5 +6
+7 +8 +9 +10

Do you stay within your recommended weight range according to your gender, age, height and general build? Do you normally use appetite suppressants? Diuretics? Thyroid medications? Have you tried crash diets? Fad diets?

Your self-evaluation is based on the following:

_____
_____

_____
_____

_____
_____

3) Exercise

-10 -9 -8 -7 -6 -5 -4 -3 -2 -1 0 +1 +2 +3 +4 +5 +6 +7 +8 +9 +10

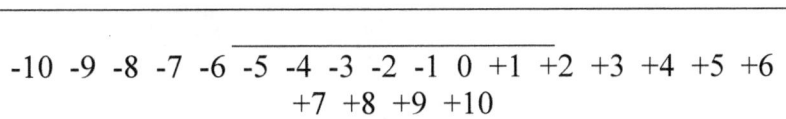

Are you involved in a regular fitness program? Is it on your own? Supervised by fitness professionals? Do you do any sports or physical activities on a routine basis for fun?

Your self-evaluation is based on the following:

_____
_____

_____
_____

_____
_____

B. Mental, Emotional Health

_____

-10 -9 -8 -7 -6 -5 -4 -3 -2 -1 0 +1 +2 +3 +4 +5 +6
+7 +8 +9 +10

How do you handle anxiety, depression, stress, or significant crises in your life? How do you handle things such as major unexpected illnesses, death, divorce, separation, or financial insecurity?

Your self-evaluation and rating are based on:

_____
_____

_____
_____

_____
_____

C. Spiritual health

-10 -9 -8 -7 -6 -5 -4 -3 -2 -1 0 +1 +2 +3 +4 +5 +6
+7 +8 +9 +10

Are you comfortable with your beliefs or absence of beliefs in a higher power? What have you done and/or what can you do to reach your own comfort level? Do you accept and respect religious beliefs different than your own?

Your rating is based on the following:

_____
_____

_____
_____

_____
_____

93

Principle II

Knowledge

An ignorant person may believe that he is truly happy. However, according to most learned people, an ignorant person is not truly happy since he is unaware of the immense possibilities for happiness that only a well-educated and knowledgeable person can experience. Humans are curious organisms by nature. Knowledge helps to satisfy curiosity about one's own self, about the world, and the universe in which we live. The better and more complete one's education, the greater measure of happiness that person should be able to achieve.

The Greek philosopher Plato defined knowledge as "justified true beliefs." Einstein said that culture is what we are left with when we have forgotten everything we learned in school.

Knowledge is actually an extremely vast concept. It is a sense of awareness with oneself, others and numerous concepts through various disciplines, mostly acquired through education. This education may be obtained in school or through formal academic institutions, or it can be self-taught through research or even through exposure to major and significant life events.

-10 -9 -8 -7 -6 -5 -4 -3 -2 -1 0 +1 +2 +3 +4 +5 +6 +7 +8 +9 +10

How would you score your overall level of knowledge? How did you acquire it? What means are you using to improve that level?

Why did you score yourself the way that you did?

_____
_____
_____
_____
_____
_____

Principle III

Social Wellness

Humans are social creatures by nature. We are not designed to be recluses or hermits. The better and more complete one's social involvement and relationships become, such as romances, friendships, or social networking, the more you will develop socially. Increased social development and adaptability lead to a greater measure of overall happiness.

1) Comfort zone within your own skin.

_____

 -10 -9 -8 -7 -6 -5 -4 -3 -2 -1 0 +1 +2 +3 +4 +5 +6
                    +7 +8 +9 +10

How comfortable are you with the way you look? Do you feel like others judge you negatively based on your appearance?

Examples of negative scores were demonstrated by a patient I met as a young woman. She was anorexic and very proud of the fact that her mother bought her clothing from the children's department. Another very attractive female patient of mine was still searching for the most famous plastic surgeons to assist her with her 6th or 7th facial surgery.

Why did you rate yourself the way you did?

_____
_____

_____
_____

_____
_____

2) Intimacy

_____

-10 -9 -8 -7 -6 -5 -4 -3 -2 -1 0 +1 +2 +3 +4 +5 +6 +7 +8 +9 +10

This indicator is seen by some as pleasurable if not wonderful. By others, it could be perceived as a duty, or even as a sinful act or a conjugal obligation. Rate your experience as positive, negative, or as one of indifference. Intimacy can even be experienced in ways other than sexual – such as spiritual or intellectual intimacy.

This is a delicate subject which is often embarrassing to discuss openly. This can be true even if you have reached a good level of intimacy with your significant other.

What are the reasons that you graded yourself as you did?

_____

_____

_____

_____

_____

_____

3) Social Life

_____
_____

-10 -9 -8 -7 -6 -5 -4 -3 -2 -1 0 +1 +2 +3 +4 +5 +6
+7 +8 +9 +10

To what extent are you satisfied with your social life? Do you have a lot of friends? Do you attend social events? Are you involved in online communities? What have you done or are you planning to do to reach a good level of satisfaction?

Explain the reasons for your rating.

97

_____

_____

_____

_____

_____

_____

4) Social Adaptability

_____

-10 -9 -8 -7 -6 -5 -4 -3 -2 -1 0 +1 +2 +3 +4
              +5 +6 +7 +8 +9 +10

When you move into a new neighborhood, town, state, or even a new country - do you find meeting new people with different backgrounds a pleasant or a difficult experience?

I remember a patient of mine who was extremely unhappy after having to move away from her home state of Pennsylvania to Arizona. She did so because her husband got an excellent job opportunity in Arizona. After several months of unsuccessful therapy for his wife, the husband had no other resources but to move back to the East Coast. There was no way for this woman to be truly happy in Arizona due a deficiency in social adaptability.

Now explain why you gave yourself the score that you did:

_____

_____

_____

_____

_____

_____

Principle IV

Character Building

"Character" refers to the total sum of traits that make up your personality. People who have low self-esteem, who feel that lack of intrinsic value, or who wish they could be someone else are generally unhappy. Most people want to be considered individuals of good character. Some of the traits that people value in themselves and in others are listed below as areas to score yourself.

Let us keep in mind that character-building is a lifelong process that requires focus and persistence. There are many components to character building. A well-built character includes a sound moral code, but it also refers to the totality of traits that make up a well-rounded person. These traits may include being educated, accomplished, and comfortable in many social settings and situations. A person with strong character will be a person with healthy self-esteem obtained by the development of one's integrity, authenticity, kindness, compassion, respect for others, tolerance and many other related qualities.

1) Authenticity

-10 -9 -8 -7 -6 -5 -4 -3 -2 -1 0 +1 +2 +3 +4 +5 +6 +7 +8 +9 +10

This is a state of being which is developed through consistent presentation of oneself, in which motives, deeds and claims are square with the truth. .

Does this following anecdote reveal a man who practices authenticity or deception? A wealthy merchant wanted a tax write-off but he also wanted to receive recognition and credit for being a philanthropist. He therefore donated a large sum of money to fund the building of a safe house for women. At the ribbon-cutting ceremony, he was asked to say a few words. In his speech, he alluded to his monetary gift as having been more than he could really afford, but he nevertheless went forward with his contribution on the grounds that he knew that women were in greater need of the safe house than he was in need of expanding his company. Was he being authentic – or deceptive?

Now write down the reasons for your rating of yourself:

_____

_____

_____

_____

_____

_____

2) Compassion, Kindness, Understanding of Others' Needs

_____

-10 -9 -8 -7 -6 -5 -4 -3 -2 -1 0 +1 +2 +3 +4 +5 +6
+7 +8 +9 +10

Compassion is a feeling of empathy for others that allows us to share their suffering and motivates our desire to help others. Compassion could be easily felt when sharing the same background (ethnic, religious, nationality). Compassion can also be expressed through donations to charitable organizations for a specific cause such as a natural disaster. Volunteering is another way to show compassion and interest in helping others in need.

Why did you rate yourself the way you did?

_____

_____

_____

_____

_____

_____

3) Integrity, Self-Honesty

_____

-10 -9 -8 -7 -6 -5 -4 -3 -2 -1 0 +1 +2 +3 +4 +5 +6
+7 +8 +9 +10

This refers to another set of strong moral principles. Integrity can also be defined as rectitude, probity, or truthfulness.

Integrity has been defined as 'what one does when no-one else is watching.'

So why did you score yourself the way that you did?

_____
_____

_____
_____

_____
_____

4) Virtue

_____

-10 -9 -8 -7 -6 -5 -4 -3 -2 -1 0 +1 +2 +3 +4 +5 +6
+7 +8 +9 +10

Today most people define "virtue" as simply moral excellence. Aristotle, however, defined a virtue as being at a point between a deficiency and an excess of a character trait. A virtue is a positive trait or quality deemed to be morally just and therefore valued as a foundation of the principles and good moral being. Personal virtues are valued as promoting collective and individual greatness. In short, "virtue" is the collective essence of one's total personality.

What are the reasons of rating yourself the way you did?

_____
_____

_____
_____

_____
_____

Principle V

Financial Resources

Financial resources are often referred to when describing the ability to obtain food, clothing, and shelter. Others include transportation means, recreation, and even health care when talking about financial resources. However, according to Aristotle, adequate financial resources are important for many other reasons. For example, finances could be a way to obtain a more adequate education, to attend trade schools, or to get closer to reaching a middle class status.

Once again, the better and more complete one is able to obtain the above (food, shelter, clothing, transportation, health care, recreation, education, and the means to develop one's cherished talents and special gifts), the greater level of happiness he will be able to reach.

Rate yourself on the financial resources to obtain the following.

1) Basic necessities, which include food, clothing, and shelter.

-10 -9 -8 -7 -6 -5 -4 -3 -2 -1 0 +1 +2 +3 +4 +5 +6 +7 +8 +9 +10

Can you afford to eat healthy foods and have a balance diet? Can you afford proper clothing adequate for different seasons? Is your habitat safe and sound and in a decent neighborhood? You could even include proper transportation means in this rating.

Your reasons to rate yourself as you did:

2) Adequate Health Care

-10 -9 -8 -7 -6 -5 -4 -3 -2 -1 0 +1 +2 +3 +4 +5 +6
+7 +8 +9 +10

Adequate health care often means being able to afford the proper medical insurance or coverage (private insurance companies, Veteran's Administration benefits, Social Security,) having access to primary care physicians and being near specialists if needed. Do you have access to hospitals, hospices, laboratory facilities and surgical procedures?

Why did you rate yourself the way you did?

_____
_____

_____
_____

_____
_____

3) Miscellaneous

_____

-10 -9 -8 -7 -6 -5 -4 -3 -2 -1 0 +1 +2 +3 +4 +5 +6
+7 +8 +9 +10

This could refer to having the means to allow your natural talents to develop and reach their full potential. An artistic wood carver or a gifted musician should be able to purchase the proper tools and instruments needed to perform in these privileged areas of expertise. Another gifted individual should be able to further his education, return or start college, or get into doctorate or fellowship programs

What are the reasons for rating yourself the way you did?

_____
_____

_____
_____

_____
_____

109

Summary Chart

Now it is time to come up with an overall average score for each of the above-described categories. Copy forward your scores for each of the following:

Physical, Mental, Emotional and Spiritual Wellness

1) Diet

_____

-10 -9 -8 -7 -6 -5 -4 -3 -2 -1 0 +1 +2 +3 +4 +5 +6
+7 +8 +9 +10

2) Weight Control

_____

-10 -9 -8 -7 -6 -5 -4 -3 -2 -1 0 +1 +2 +3 +4 +5 +6
+7 +8 +9 +10

3) Exercise

_____

-10 -9 -8 -7 -6 -5 -4 -3 -2 -1 0 +1 +2 +3 +4 +5 +6
+7 +8 +9 +10

4) Mental and Emotional Health

_____

-10 -9 -8 -7 -6 -5 -4 -3 -2 -1 0 +1 +2 +3 +4 +5 +6
+7 +8 +9 +10

5) Spiritual Health

_____

-10 -9 -8 -7 -6 -5 -4 -3 -2 -1 0 +1 +2 +3 +4 +5 +6
+7 +8 +9 +10

Now add up your scores for these five categories. Your total
score will be somewhere between -50 and +50. Divide that
total score by 5 to find out your average score for Physical,
Mental, Emotional and Spiritual Wellness that will be between
-10 and +10.

Record your average score here: _____
Date: _____

Knowledge

1) Knowledge

_____

-10 -9 -8 -7 -6 -5 -4 -3 -2 -1 0 +1 +2 +3 +4 +5 +6
+7 +8 +9 +10

Since there is only one score in the 'Knowledge' category, this
number will also be your average score.

111

Record your average score here: _____

Date: _____

Social Wellness

1) Comfort Zone

_____

-10 -9 -8 -7 -6 -5 -4 -3 -2 -1 0 +1 +2 +3 +4 +5 +6
+7 +8 +9 +10

2) Intimacy

_____

-10 -9 -8 -7 -6 -5 -4 -3 -2 -1 0 +1 +2 +3 +4 +5 +6
+7 +8 +9 +10

3) Social Life

_____

-10 -9 -8 -7 -6 -5 -4 -3 -2 -1 0 +1 +2 +3 +4 +5 +6 +7 +8 +9
+10

4) Social Adaptability

-10 -9 -8 -7 -6 -5 -4 -3 -2 -1 0 +1 +2 +3 +4 +5 +6 +7 +8 +9 +10

Your total score for these four categories should fall between -40 and + 40. Divide that total score by 4 in order to reach an average score for Social Wellness between -10 and +10.

Record your average score here: _____
Date: _____

Character Building

1) Authenticity

-10 -9 -8 -7 -6 -5 -4 -3 -2 -1 0 +1 +2 +3 +4 +5 +6 +7 +8 +9 +10

2) Compassion, Kindness, Understanding of Others' Needs

-10 -9 -8 -7 -6 -5 -4 -3 -2 -1 0 +1 +2 +3 +4 +5 +6 +7 +8 +9 +10

3) Integrity, Self-Honesty

-10 -9 -8 -7 -6 -5 -4 -3 -2 -1 0 +1 +2 +3 +4 +5 +6 +7 +8 +9 +10

4) Virtue

113

-10 -9 -8 -7 -6 -5 -4 -3 -2 -1 0 +1 +2 +3 +4 +5 +6
+7 +8 +9 +10

Once again, add up your four totals for this category for a total between -40 and +40. Divide this number by 4 to find your average score for Character Building which will be between -10 and +10.

Record your average score here: _____
Date: _____

Financial Resources

1) Basic Necessities

-10 -9 -8 -7 -6 -5 -4 -3 -2 -1 0 +1 +2 +3 +4 +5 +6
+7 +8 +9 +10

2) Adequate Health Care

-10 -9 -8 -7 -6 -5 -4 -3 -2 -1 0 +1 +2 +3 +4 +5 +6
+7 +8 +9 +10

3) Miscellaneous

-10 -9 -8 -7 -6 -5 -4 -3 -2 -1 0 +1 +2 +3 +4 +5 +6
+7 +8 +9 +10

For this final category, add up your three scores for a total that will be between -30 and +30. Divide this score by 3 to come up with an average Financial Resources score between -10 and +10.

Record your average score here: _____
Date: _____

SET NUMBER TWO

Principle I

Physical, Mental, Emotional and Spiritual Wellness

The better and more complete your physical, mental, emotional and spiritual health becomes, the greater the measure of happiness you will achieve in life. When our lives are plagued by chronic illnesses, and aches and pains, or if we happen to be constantly vulnerable to the common cold or other ailments, our morale deteriorates and so does our delight in life.

Being constantly out of sorts is often the result of some physical problems that can easily be remedied. The worst thing to do is to do nothing. The first thing we ought to do is to get a proper medical diagnosis. If nothing can be done to relieve a medical issue, then our task is to learn to accept that which cannot be changed, to adapt to some limitations of our activity level, and eventually compensate for those limitations in other areas of our lives.

One example of this kind of compensation and adaptation is illustrated by the famous impressionist painter, Renoir. In his last 25 years of his active artistic life, he suffered from debilitating arthritis. His passion for painting, including 400 hundred masterpieces in his last 10 years, did not subside with his physical limitations. Instead, he tied his brushes to his hands and arms since he was unable to hold them tightly. He also found and developed sophisticated ways to access his easels.

116

Another much younger artist became extremely depressed all the way to the point of considering suicide. He had found out that his severe retinal deterioration was going to prevent him from finishing 25 paintings that he was scheduled to show in a local art gallery. Therapeutic intervention helped him to realize that he could still enjoy a few more months of his artistic creativity rather than focus on the quantity of paintings he could produce.

Yet another example of this phenomenon was demonstrated by a personal patient of mine. He was a very bright man in his mid-fifties, but he was becoming very depressed as he realized he could no longer run his normal five miles every morning. Through some short term individual therapy, he was able to accept the fact that some physiological changes had gradually occurred. He also discovered that 2 miles of daily jogging could be just as enjoyable and with a lot less pain. He had the option to lament and get more depressed, but instead he refused to give in to his gradually worsening limitations.

Following the instructions provided in the last section, it is time to rate yourself on the following elements that affect your general wellness.

A. Physical Health

1) Diet

-10 -9 -8 -7 -6 -5 -4 -3 -2 -1 0 +1 +2 +3 +4 +5 +6 +7 +8 +9 +10

Do you eat a balanced diet? How often do you indulge in "junk food"? Does your diet include fruits? Green vegetables? Excessive amounts of meat? Do you use excessive amounts of caffeine? Artificial sweeteners? Tobacco? Appetite suppressants?

Why did you rate yourself the way you did about your diet?

_____

_____

_____

_____

_____

_____

2) Weight control

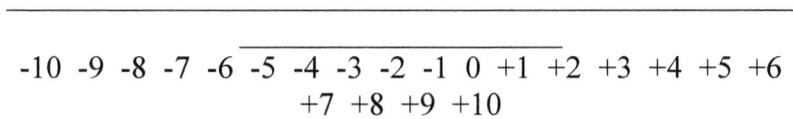

$$-10 \ -9 \ -8 \ -7 \ -6 \ -5 \ -4 \ -3 \ -2 \ -1 \ 0 \ +1 \ +2 \ +3 \ +4 \ +5 \ +6$$
$$+7 \ +8 \ +9 \ +10$$

Do you stay within your recommended weight range according to your gender, age, height and general build? Do you normally use appetite suppressants? Diuretics? Thyroid medications? Have you tried crash diets? Fad diets?

Your self-evaluation is based on the following:

_____
_____

_____
_____

_____
_____

3) Exercise

-10 -9 -8 -7 -6 -5 -4 -3 -2 -1 0 +1 +2 +3 +4 +5 +6 +7 +8 +9 +10

Are you involved in a regular fitness program? Is it on your own? Supervised by fitness professionals? Do you do any sports or physical activities on a routine basis for fun?

Your self-evaluation is based on the following:

_____

_____

_____

_____

_____

_____

B. Mental, Emotional Health

_____

-10 -9 -8 -7 -6 -5 -4 -3 -2 -1 0 +1 +2 +3 +4 +5 +6
+7 +8 +9 +10

How do you handle anxiety, depression, stress, or significant crises in your life? How do you handle things such as major unexpected illnesses, death, divorce, separation, or financial insecurity?

Your self-evaluation and rating are based on:

_____
_____

_____
_____

_____
_____

C. Spiritual health

_____

-10 -9 -8 -7 -6 -5 -4 -3 -2 -1 0 +1 +2 +3 +4 +5 +6
+7 +8 +9 +10

Are you comfortable with your beliefs or absence of beliefs in a higher power? What have you done and/or what can you do to reach your own comfort level? Do you accept and respect religious beliefs different than your own?

Your rating is based on the following:

_____
_____

_____
_____

_____
_____

Principle II

Knowledge

An ignorant person may believe that he is truly happy. However, according to most learned people, an ignorant person is not truly happy since he is unaware of the immense possibilities for happiness that only a well-educated and knowledgeable person can experience. Humans are curious organisms by nature. Knowledge helps to satisfy curiosity about one's own self, about the world, and the universe in which we live. The better and more complete one's education, the greater measure of happiness that person should be able to achieve.

The Greek philosopher Plato defined knowledge as "justified true beliefs." Einstein said that culture is what we are left with when we have forgotten everything we learned in school.

Knowledge is actually an extremely vast concept. It is a sense of awareness with oneself, others and numerous concepts through various disciplines, mostly acquired through education. This education may be obtained in school or through formal academic institutions, or it can be self-taught through research or even through exposure to major and significant life events.

-10 -9 -8 -7 -6 -5 -4 -3 -2 -1 0 +1 +2 +3 +4 +5 +6 +7 +8 +9 +10

How would you score your overall level of knowledge? How did you acquire it? What means are you using to improve that level?

Why did you score yourself the way that you did?

_____

_____

_____

_____

_____

_____

Principle III

Social Wellness

Humans are social creatures by nature. We are not designed to be recluses or hermits. The better and more complete one's social involvement and relationships become, such as romances, friendships, or social networking, the more you will develop socially. Increased social development and adaptability lead to a greater measure of overall happiness.

2) Comfort zone within your own skin.

_____

-10 -9 -8 -7 -6 -5 -4 -3 -2 -1 0 +1 +2 +3 +4 +5 +6
+7 +8 +9 +10

How comfortable are you with the way you look? Do you feel like others judge you negatively based on your appearance?

Examples of negative scores were demonstrated by a patient I met as a young woman. She was anorexic and very proud of the fact that her mother bought her clothing from the children's department. Another very attractive female patient of mine was still searching for the most famous plastic surgeons to assist her with her 6th or 7th facial surgery.

Why did you rate yourself the way you did?

_____

_____

_____

_____

_____

_____

2) Intimacy

_____

-10 -9 -8 -7 -6 -5 -4 -3 -2 -1 0 +1 +2 +3 +4 +5 +6 +7 +8 +9 +10

This indicator is seen by some as pleasurable if not wonderful. By others, it could be perceived as a duty, or even as a sinful act or a conjugal obligation. Rate your experience as positive, negative, or as one of indifference. Intimacy can even be experienced in ways other than sexual – such as spiritual or intellectual intimacy.

This is a delicate subject which is often embarrassing to discuss openly. This can be true even if you have reached a good level of intimacy with your significant other.

What are the reasons that you graded yourself as you did?

_____
_____

_____
_____

_____
_____

3) Social Life

_____

-10 -9 -8 -7 -6 -5 -4 -3 -2 -1 0 +1 +2 +3 +4 +5 +6
+7 +8 +9 +10

To what extent are you satisfied with your social life? Do you have a lot of friends? Do you attend social events? Are you involved in online communities? What have you done or are you planning to do to reach a good level of satisfaction?

Explain the reasons for your rating.

_____
_____

_____
_____

_____
_____

4) Social Adaptability

_____
        _____
 -10 -9 -8 -7 -6 -5 -4 -3 -2 -1 0 +1 +2 +3 +4
              +5 +6 +7 +8 +9 +10

When you move into a new neighborhood, town, state, or even a new country - do you find meeting new people with different backgrounds a pleasant or a difficult experience?

I remember a patient of mine who was extremely unhappy after having to move away from her home state of Pennsylvania to Arizona. She did so because her husband got an excellent job opportunity in Arizona. After several months of unsuccessful therapy for his wife, the husband had no other resources but to move back to the East Coast. There was no way for this woman to be truly happy in Arizona due a deficiency in social adaptability.

127

Now explain why you gave yourself the score that you did:

_____

_____

_____

_____

_____

_____

Principle IV

Character Building

"Character" refers to the total sum of traits that make up your personality. People who have low self-esteem, who feel that lack of intrinsic value, or who wish they could be someone else are generally unhappy. Most people want to be considered individuals of good character. Some of the traits that people value in themselves and in others are listed below as areas to score yourself.

Let us keep in mind that character-building is a lifelong process that requires focus and persistence. There are many components to character building. A well-built character includes a sound moral code, but it also refers to the totality of traits that make up a well-rounded person. These traits may include being educated, accomplished, and comfortable in many social settings and situations. A person with strong character will be a person with healthy self-esteem obtained by the development of one's integrity, authenticity, kindness, compassion, respect for others, tolerance and many other related qualities.

1) Authenticity

-10 -9 -8 -7 -6 -5 -4 -3 -2 -1 0 +1 +2 +3 +4 +5 +6 +7 +8 +9 +10

This is a state of being which is developed through consistent presentation of oneself, in which motives, deeds and claims are square with the truth. .

Does this following anecdote reveal a man who practices authenticity or deception? A wealthy merchant wanted a tax write-off but he also wanted to receive recognition and credit for being a philanthropist. He therefore donated a large sum of money to fund the building of a safe house for women. At the ribbon-cutting ceremony, he was asked to say a few words. In his speech, he alluded to his monetary gift as having been more than he could really afford, but he nevertheless went forward with his contribution on the grounds that he knew that women were in greater need of the safe house than he was in need of expanding his company. Was he being authentic – or deceptive?

Now write down the reasons for your rating of yourself:

_____

_____

_____

_____

_____

_____

2) Compassion, Kindness, Understanding of Others' Needs

_____

-10 -9 -8 -7 -6 -5 -4 -3 -2 -1 0 +1 +2 +3 +4 +5 +6
+7 +8 +9 +10

Compassion is a feeling of empathy for others that allows us to share their suffering and motivates our desire to help others. Compassion could be easily felt when sharing the same background (ethnic, religious, nationality). Compassion can also be expressed through donations to charitable organizations for a specific cause such as a natural disaster. Volunteering is another way to show compassion and interest in helping others in need.

Why did you rate yourself the way you did?

_____

_____

_____

_____

_____

_____

3) Integrity, Self-Honesty

_____

-10 -9 -8 -7 -6 -5 -4 -3 -2 -1 0 +1 +2 +3 +4 +5 +6
+7 +8 +9 +10

This refers to another set of strong moral principles. Integrity can also be defined as rectitude, probity, or truthfulness. Integrity has been defined as 'what one does when no-one else is watching.'

So why did you score yourself the way that you did?

_____
_____

_____
_____

_____
_____

4) Virtue

-10 -9 -8 -7 -6 -5 -4 -3 -2 -1 0 +1 +2 +3 +4 +5 +6
+7 +8 +9 +10

Today most people define "virtue" as simply moral excellence. Aristotle, however, defined a virtue as being at a point between a deficiency and an excess of a character trait. A virtue is a positive trait or quality deemed to be morally just and therefore valued as a foundation of the principles and good moral being. Personal virtues are valued as promoting collective and individual greatness. In short, "virtue" is the collective essence of one's total personality.

What are the reasons of rating yourself the way you did?

Principle V

Financial Resources

Financial resources are often referred to when describing the ability to obtain food, clothing, and shelter. Others include transportation means, recreation, and even health care when talking about financial resources. However, according to Aristotle, adequate financial resources are important for many other reasons. For example, finances could be a way to obtain a more adequate education, to attend trade schools, or to get closer to reaching a middle class status.

Once again, the better and more complete one is able to obtain the above (food, shelter, clothing, transportation, health care, recreation, education, and the means to develop one's cherished talents and special gifts), the greater level of happiness he will be able to reach.

Rate yourself on the financial resources to obtain the following.

2) Basic necessities, which include food, clothing, and shelter.

_____

-10 -9 -8 -7 -6 -5 -4 -3 -2 -1 0 +1 +2 +3 +4 +5 +6
+7 +8 +9 +10

Can you afford to eat healthy foods and have a balance diet? Can you afford proper clothing adequate for different seasons? Is your habitat safe and sound and in a decent neighborhood? You could even include proper transportation means in this rating.

Your reasons to rate yourself as you did:

_____
_____

_____
_____

_____
_____

2) Adequate Health Care

_____

-10 -9 -8 -7 -6 -5 -4 -3 -2 -1 0 +1 +2 +3 +4 +5 +6
+7 +8 +9 +10

Adequate health care often means being able to afford the proper medical insurance or coverage (private insurance companies, Veteran's Administration benefits, Social Security,) having access to primary care physicians and being near specialists if needed. Do you have access to hospitals, hospices, laboratory facilities and surgical procedures?

Why did you rate yourself the way you did?

_____
_____

_____
_____

_____
_____

3) Miscellaneous

_____

-10 -9 -8 -7 -6 -5 -4 -3 -2 -1 0 +1 +2 +3 +4 +5 +6
+7 +8 +9 +10

This could refer to having the means to allow your natural talents to develop and reach their full potential. An artistic wood carver or a gifted musician should be able to purchase the proper tools and instruments needed to perform in these privileged areas of expertise. Another gifted individual should be able to further his education, return or start college, or get into doctorate or fellowship programs

What are the reasons for rating yourself the way you did?

_____
_____

_____
_____

_____
_____

137

Summary Chart

Now it is time to come up with an overall average score for each of the above-described categories. Copy forward your scores for each of the following:

<u>Physical, Mental, Emotional and Spiritual Wellness</u>

6) Diet

_____

-10 -9 -8 -7 -6 -5 -4 -3 -2 -1 0 +1 +2 +3 +4 +5 +6 +7 +8 +9 +10

7) Weight Control

_____

-10 -9 -8 -7 -6 -5 -4 -3 -2 -1 0 +1 +2 +3 +4 +5 +6 +7 +8 +9 +10

8) Exercise

_____

-10 -9 -8 -7 -6 -5 -4 -3 -2 -1 0 +1 +2 +3 +4 +5 +6 +7 +8 +9 +10

9) Mental and Emotional Health

_____

-10 -9 -8 -7 -6 -5 -4 -3 -2 -1 0 +1 +2 +3 +4 +5 +6 +7 +8 +9 +10

10) Spiritual Health

-10 -9 -8 -7 -6 -5 -4 -3 -2 -1 0 +1 +2 +3 +4 +5 +6
+7 +8 +9 +10

Now add up your scores for these five categories. Your total score will be somewhere between -50 and +50. Divide that total score by 5 to find out your average score for Physical, Mental, Emotional and Spiritual Wellness that will be between -10 and +10.

Record your average score here: _____
Date: _____

Knowledge

5) Knowledge

_____

-10 -9 -8 -7 -6 -5 -4 -3 -2 -1 0 +1 +2 +3 +4 +5 +6
+7 +8 +9 +10

Since there is only one score in the 'Knowledge' category, this number will also be your average score.

Record your average score here: _____
Date: _____

139

Social Wellness

1) Comfort Zone

-10 -9 -8 -7 -6 -5 -4 -3 -2 -1 0 +1 +2 +3 +4 +5 +6 +7 +8 +9 +10

6) Intimacy

-10 -9 -8 -7 -6 -5 -4 -3 -2 -1 0 +1 +2 +3 +4 +5 +6 +7 +8 +9 +10

7) Social Life

-10 -9 -8 -7 -6 -5 -4 -3 -2 -1 0 +1 +2 +3 +4 +5 +6 +7 +8 +9 +10

8) Social Adaptability

-10 -9 -8 -7 -6 -5 -4 -3 -2 -1 0 +1 +2 +3 +4 +5 +6 +7 +8 +9 +10

Your total score for these four categories should fall between -40 and + 40. Divide that total score by 4 in order to reach an average score for Social Wellness between -10 and +10.

Record your average score here: _____
Date: _____

Character Building

1) Authenticity

_____

-10 -9 -8 -7 -6 -5 -4 -3 -2 -1 0 +1 +2 +3 +4 +5 +6
+7 +8 +9 +10

2) Compassion, Kindness, Understanding of Others' Needs

_____

-10 -9 -8 -7 -6 -5 -4 -3 -2 -1 0 +1 +2 +3 +4 +5 +6
+7 +8 +9 +10

3) Integrity, Self-Honesty

_____

-10 -9 -8 -7 -6 -5 -4 -3 -2 -1 0 +1 +2 +3 +4 +5 +6
+7 +8 +9 +10

4) Virtue

_____

-10 -9 -8 -7 -6 -5 -4 -3 -2 -1 0 +1 +2 +3 +4 +5 +6
+7 +8 +9 +10

Once again, add up your four totals for this category for a total between -40 and +40. Divide this number by 4 to find your average score for Character Building which will be between -10 and +10.

Record your average score here: _____
Date: _____

Financial Resources

1) Basic Necessities

_____

-10 -9 -8 -7 -6 -5 -4 -3 -2 -1 0 +1 +2 +3 +4 +5 +6
+7 +8 +9 +10

2) Adequate Health Care

_____

-10 -9 -8 -7 -6 -5 -4 -3 -2 -1 0 +1 +2 +3 +4 +5 +6
+7 +8 +9 +10

3) Miscellaneous

_____

-10 -9 -8 -7 -6 -5 -4 -3 -2 -1 0 +1 +2 +3 +4 +5 +6
+7 +8 +9 +10

For this final category, add up your three scores for a total that will be between -30 and +30. Divide this score by 3 to come up with an average Financial Resources score between -10 and +10.

Record your average score here: _____

Date: _____

SET NUMBER THREE

Principle I

Physical, Mental, Emotional and Spiritual Wellness

The better and more complete your physical, mental, emotional and spiritual health becomes, the greater the measure of happiness you will achieve in life. When our lives are plagued by chronic illnesses, and aches and pains, or if we happen to be constantly vulnerable to the common cold or other ailments, our morale deteriorates and so does our delight in life.

Being constantly out of sorts is often the result of some physical problems that can easily be remedied. The worst thing to do is to do nothing. The first thing we ought to do is to get a proper medical diagnosis. If nothing can be done to relieve a medical issue, then our task is to learn to accept that which cannot be changed, to adapt to some limitations of our activity level, and eventually compensate for those limitations in other areas of our lives.

One example of this kind of compensation and adaptation is illustrated by the famous impressionist painter, Renoir. In his last 25 years of his active artistic life, he suffered from debilitating arthritis. His passion for painting, including 400 hundred masterpieces in his last 10 years, did not subside with his physical limitations. Instead, he tied his brushes to his hands and arms since he was unable to hold them tightly. He also found and developed sophisticated ways to access his easels.

Another much younger artist became extremely depressed all the way to the point of considering suicide. He had found out that his severe retinal deterioration was going to prevent him from finishing 25 paintings that he was scheduled to show in a local art gallery. Therapeutic intervention helped him to realize that he could still enjoy a few more months of his artistic creativity rather than focus on the quantity of paintings he could produce.

Yet another example of this phenomenon was demonstrated by a personal patient of mine. He was a very bright man in his mid-fifties, but he was becoming very depressed as he realized he could no longer run his normal five miles every morning. Through some short term individual therapy, he was able to accept the fact that some physiological changes had gradually occurred. He also discovered that 2 miles of daily jogging could be just as enjoyable and with a lot less pain. He had the option to lament and get more depressed, but instead he refused to give in to his gradually worsening limitations.

Following the instructions provided in the last section, it is time to rate yourself on the following elements that affect your general wellness.

A. Physical Health

1) Diet

_____

-10 -9 -8 -7 -6 -5 -4 -3 -2 -1 0 +1 +2 +3 +4 +5 +6
+7 +8 +9 +10

Do you eat a balanced diet? How often do you indulge in "junk food"? Does your diet include fruits? Green vegetables? Excessive amounts of meat? Do you use excessive amounts of caffeine? Artificial sweeteners? Tobacco? Appetite suppressants?

Why did you rate yourself the way you did about your diet?

_____
_____

_____
_____

_____
_____

2) Weight control

_____

_____
-10 -9 -8 -7 -6 -5 -4 -3 -2 -1 0 +1 +2 +3 +4 +5 +6
+7 +8 +9 +10

Do you stay within your recommended weight range according to your gender, age, height and general build? Do you normally use appetite suppressants? Diuretics? Thyroid medications? Have you tried crash diets? Fad diets?

Your self-evaluation is based on the following:

_____
_____

_____
_____

_____
_____

147

3) Exercise

-10 -9 -8 -7 -6 -5 -4 -3 -2 -1 0 +1 +2 +3 +4 +5 +6
+7 +8 +9 +10

Are you involved in a regular fitness program? Is it on your own? Supervised by fitness professionals? Do you do any sports or physical activities on a routine basis for fun?

Your self-evaluation is based on the following:

_____
_____

_____
_____

_____
_____

B. Mental, Emotional Health

-10 -9 -8 -7 -6 -5 -4 -3 -2 -1 0 +1 +2 +3 +4 +5 +6
+7 +8 +9 +10

How do you handle anxiety, depression, stress, or significant crises in your life? How do you handle things such as major unexpected illnesses, death, divorce, separation, or financial insecurity?

Your self-evaluation and rating are based on:

_____
_____

_____
_____

_____
_____

C. Spiritual health

-10 -9 -8 -7 -6 -5 -4 -3 -2 -1 0 +1 +2 +3 +4 +5 +6
+7 +8 +9 +10

Are you comfortable with your beliefs or absence of beliefs in a higher power? What have you done and/or what can you do to reach your own comfort level? Do you accept and respect religious beliefs different than your own?

Your rating is based on the following:

_____
_____

_____
_____

_____
_____

Principle II

Knowledge

An ignorant person may believe that he is truly happy. However, according to most learned people, an ignorant person is not truly happy since he is unaware of the immense possibilities for happiness that only a well-educated and knowledgeable person can experience. Humans are curious organisms by nature. Knowledge helps to satisfy curiosity about one's own self, about the world, and the universe in which we live. The better and more complete one's education, the greater measure of happiness that person should be able to achieve.

The Greek philosopher Plato defined knowledge as "justified true beliefs." Einstein said that culture is what we are left with when we have forgotten everything we learned in school.

Knowledge is actually an extremely vast concept. It is a sense of awareness with oneself, others and numerous concepts through various disciplines, mostly acquired through education. This education may be obtained in school or through formal academic institutions, or it can be self-taught through research or even through exposure to major and significant life events.

-10 -9 -8 -7 -6 -5 -4 -3 -2 -1 0 +1 +2 +3 +4 +5 +6 +7 +8 +9 +10

How would you score your overall level of knowledge? How did you acquire it? What means are you using to improve that level?

151

Why did you score yourself the way that you did?

_____

_____

_____

_____

_____

_____

Principle III

Social Wellness

Humans are social creatures by nature. We are not designed to be recluses or hermits. The better and more complete one's social involvement and relationships become, such as romances, friendships, or social networking, the more you will develop socially. Increased social development and adaptability lead to a greater measure of overall happiness.

3) Comfort zone within your own skin.

_____

 -10 -9 -8 -7 -6 -5 -4 -3 -2 -1 0 +1 +2 +3 +4 +5 +6
+7 +8 +9 +10

How comfortable are you with the way you look? Do you feel like others judge you negatively based on your appearance?

Examples of negative scores were demonstrated by a patient I met as a young woman. She was anorexic and very proud of the fact that her mother bought her clothing from the children's department. Another very attractive female patient of mine was still searching for the most famous plastic surgeons to assist her with her 6th or 7th facial surgery.

Why did you rate yourself the way you did?

_____

_____

_____

_____

_____

_____

2) Intimacy

_____

-10 -9 -8 -7 -6 -5 -4 -3 -2 -1 0 +1 +2 +3 +4 +5 +6
+7 +8 +9 +10

This indicator is seen by some as pleasurable if not wonderful. By others, it could be perceived as a duty, or even as a sinful act or a conjugal obligation. Rate your experience as positive, negative, or as one of indifference. Intimacy can even be experienced in ways other than sexual – such as spiritual or intellectual intimacy.

153

This is a delicate subject which is often embarrassing to discuss openly. This can be true even if you have reached a good level of intimacy with your significant other.

What are the reasons that you graded yourself as you did?

_____
_____

_____
_____

_____
_____

3) Social Life

_____
_____

-10 -9 -8 -7 -6 -5 -4 -3 -2 -1 0 +1 +2 +3 +4 +5 +6
+7 +8 +9 +10

To what extent are you satisfied with your social life? Do you have a lot of friends? Do you attend social events? Are you involved in online communities? What have you done or are you planning to do to reach a good level of satisfaction?

154

Explain the reasons for your rating.

_____
_____

_____
_____

_____
_____

4) Social Adaptability

_____
                    _____
-10 -9 -8 -7 -6 -5 -4 -3 -2 -1 0 +1 +2 +3 +4
              +5 +6 +7 +8 +9 +10

When you move into a new neighborhood, town, state, or even a new country - do you find meeting new people with different backgrounds a pleasant or a difficult experience?

I remember a patient of mine who was extremely unhappy after having to move away from her home state of Pennsylvania to Arizona. She did so because her husband got an excellent job opportunity in Arizona. After several months of unsuccessful therapy for his wife, the husband had no other resources but to move back to the East Coast. There was no way for this woman to be truly happy in Arizona due a deficiency in social adaptability.

155

Now explain why you gave yourself the score that you did:

_____
_____

_____
_____

_____
_____

Principle IV

Character Building

"Character" refers to the total sum of traits that make up your personality. People who have low self-esteem, who feel that lack of intrinsic value, or who wish they could be someone else are generally unhappy. Most people want to be considered individuals of good character. Some of the traits that people value in themselves and in others are listed below as areas to score yourself.

Let us keep in mind that character-building is a lifelong process that requires focus and persistence. There are many components to character building. A well-built character includes a sound moral code, but it also refers to the totality of traits that make up a well-rounded person. These traits may include being educated, accomplished, and comfortable in many social settings and situations. A person with strong character will be a person with healthy self-esteem obtained by the development of one's integrity, authenticity, kindness, compassion, respect for others, tolerance and many other related qualities.

1) Authenticity

-10 -9 -8 -7 -6 -5 -4 -3 -2 -1 0 +1 +2 +3 +4 +5 +6
+7 +8 +9 +10

This is a state of being which is developed through consistent presentation of oneself, in which motives, deeds and claims are square with the truth. .

Does this following anecdote reveal a man who practices authenticity or deception? A wealthy merchant wanted a tax write-off but he also wanted to receive recognition and credit for being a philanthropist. He therefore donated a large sum of money to fund the building of a safe house for women. At the ribbon-cutting ceremony, he was asked to say a few words. In his speech, he alluded to his monetary gift as having been more than he could really afford, but he nevertheless went forward with his contribution on the grounds that he knew that women were in greater need of the safe house than he was in need of expanding his company. Was he being authentic – or deceptive?

Now write down the reasons for your rating of yourself:

_____
_____

_____
_____

_____
_____

2) Compassion, Kindness, Understanding of Others' Needs

_____

-10 -9 -8 -7 -6 -5 -4 -3 -2 -1 0 +1 +2 +3 +4 +5 +6
+7 +8 +9 +10

Compassion is a feeling of empathy for others that allows us to share their suffering and motivates our desire to help others. Compassion could be easily felt when sharing the same background (ethnic, religious, nationality). Compassion can also be expressed through donations to charitable organizations for a specific cause such as a natural disaster. Volunteering is another way to show compassion and interest in helping others in need.

Why did you rate yourself the way you did?

_____
_____

_____
_____

_____
_____

159

3) Integrity, Self-Honesty

_____

-10 -9 -8 -7 -6 -5 -4 -3 -2 -1 0 +1 +2 +3 +4 +5 +6
+7 +8 +9 +10

This refers to another set of strong moral principles. Integrity can also be defined as rectitude, probity, or truthfulness. Integrity has been defined as 'what one does when no-one else is watching.'

So why did you score yourself the way that you did?

_____
_____

_____
_____

_____
_____

4) Virtue

-10 -9 -8 -7 -6 -5 -4 -3 -2 -1 0 +1 +2 +3 +4 +5 +6
+7 +8 +9 +10

Today most people define "virtue" as simply moral excellence. Aristotle, however, defined a virtue as being at a point between a deficiency and an excess of a character trait. A virtue is a positive trait or quality deemed to be morally just and therefore valued as a foundation of the principles and good moral being. Personal virtues are valued as promoting collective and individual greatness. In short, "virtue" is the collective essence of one's total personality.

What are the reasons of rating yourself the way you did?

_____

_____

_____

_____

_____

_____

Principle V

Financial Resources

Financial resources are often referred to when describing the ability to obtain food, clothing, and shelter. Others include transportation means, recreation, and even health care when talking about financial resources. However, according to Aristotle, adequate financial resources are important for many other reasons. For example, finances could be a way to obtain a more adequate education, to attend trade schools, or to get closer to reaching a middle class status.

Once again, the better and more complete one is able to obtain the above (food, shelter, clothing, transportation, health care, recreation, education, and the means to develop one's cherished talents and special gifts), the greater level of happiness he will be able to reach.

Rate yourself on the financial resources to obtain the following.

3) Basic necessities, which include food, clothing, and shelter.

_____

-10 -9 -8 -7 -6 -5 -4 -3 -2 -1 0 +1 +2 +3 +4 +5 +6
+7 +8 +9 +10

Can you afford to eat healthy foods and have a balance diet? Can you afford proper clothing adequate for different seasons? Is your habitat safe and sound and in a decent neighborhood? You could even include proper transportation means in this rating.

Your reasons to rate yourself as you did:

_____
_____

_____
_____

_____
_____

163

2) Adequate Health Care

_____

-10 -9 -8 -7 -6 -5 -4 -3 -2 -1 0 +1 +2 +3 +4 +5 +6
+7 +8 +9 +10

Adequate health care often means being able to afford the
proper medical insurance or coverage (private insurance
companies, Veteran's Administration benefits, Social
Security,) having access to primary care physicians and being
near specialists if needed. Do you have access to hospitals,
hospices, laboratory facilities and surgical procedures?

Why did you rate yourself the way you did?

_____
_____

_____
_____

_____
_____

3) Miscellaneous

‒_____

-10 -9 -8 -7 -6 ‾-5‾ -4 -3 -2 -1 0 +1 +2 +3 +4 +5 +6
+7 +8 +9 +10

This could refer to having the means to allow your natural talents to develop and reach their full potential. An artistic wood carver or a gifted musician should be able to purchase the proper tools and instruments needed to perform in these privileged areas of expertise. Another gifted individual should be able to further his education, return or start college, or get into doctorate or fellowship programs

What are the reasons for rating yourself the way you did?

_____
_____

_____
_____

_____
_____

Summary Chart

Now it is time to come up with an overall average score for each of the above-described categories. Copy forward your scores for each of the following:

<u>Physical, Mental, Emotional and Spiritual Wellness</u>

11) Diet

_____

-10 -9 -8 -7 -6 -5 -4 -3 -2 -1 0 +1 +2 +3 +4 +5 +6
+7 +8 +9 +10

12) Weight Control

_____

-10 -9 -8 -7 -6 -5 -4 -3 -2 -1 0 +1 +2 +3 +4 +5 +6
+7 +8 +9 +10

13) Exercise

_____

-10 -9 -8 -7 -6 -5 -4 -3 -2 -1 0 +1 +2 +3 +4 +5 +6
+7 +8 +9 +10

14) Mental and Emotional Health

_____

-10 -9 -8 -7 -6 -5 -4 -3 -2 -1 0 +1 +2 +3 +4 +5 +6
+7 +8 +9 +10

15) Spiritual Health

-10 -9 -8 -7 -6 -5 -4 -3 -2 -1 0 +1 +2 +3 +4 +5 +6
+7 +8 +9 +10

Now add up your scores for these five categories. Your total score will be somewhere between -50 and +50. Divide that total score by 5 to find out your average score for Physical, Mental, Emotional and Spiritual Wellness that will be between -10 and +10.

Record your average score here: _____
Date: _____

Knowledge

9) Knowledge

-10 -9 -8 -7 -6 -5 -4 -3 -2 -1 0 +1 +2 +3 +4 +5 +6
+7 +8 +9 +10

Since there is only one score in the 'Knowledge' category, this number will also be your average score.

167

Record your average score here: _____

Date: _____

Social Wellness

1) Comfort Zone

_____

-10 -9 -8 -7 -6 -5 -4 -3 -2 -1 0 +1 +2 +3 +4 +5 +6
+7 +8 +9 +10

10) Intimacy

_____

-10 -9 -8 -7 -6 -5 -4 -3 -2 -1 0 +1 +2 +3 +4 +5 +6
+7 +8 +9 +10

11) Social Life

_____

-10 -9 -8 -7 -6 -5 -4 -3 -2 -1 0 +1 +2 +3 +4 +5 +6 +7 +8 +9
+10

168

12) Social Adaptability

_____

-10 -9 -8 -7 -6 -5 -4 -3 -2 -1 0 +1 +2 +3 +4 +5 +6 +7 +8 +9
+10

Your total score for these four categories should fall between
-40 and + 40. Divide that total score by 4 in order to reach an
average score for Social Wellness between -10 and +10.

Record your average score here: _____
Date: _____

<u>Character Building</u>

1) Authenticity

_____

-10 -9 -8 -7 -6 -5 -4 -3 -2 -1 0 +1 +2 +3 +4 +5 +6
+7 +8 +9 +10

2) Compassion, Kindness, Understanding of Others' Needs

_____

-10 -9 -8 -7 -6 -5 -4 -3 -2 -1 0 +1 +2 +3 +4 +5 +6
+7 +8 +9 +10

3) Integrity, Self-Honesty

_____

-10 -9 -8 -7 -6 -5 -4 -3 -2 -1 0 +1 +2 +3 +4 +5 +6
+7 +8 +9 +10

4) Virtue

_____

-10 -9 -8 -7 -6 -5 -4 -3 -2 -1 0 +1 +2 +3 +4 +5 +6
+7 +8 +9 +10

Once again, add up your four totals for this category for a total between -40 and +40. Divide this number by 4 to find your average score for Character Building which will be between -10 and +10.

Record your average score here: _____
Date: _____

Financial Resources

1) Basic Necessities

_____

-10 -9 -8 -7 -6 -5 -4 -3 -2 -1 0 +1 +2 +3 +4 +5 +6
+7 +8 +9 +10

2) Adequate Health Care

_____

-10 -9 -8 -7 -6 -5 -4 -3 -2 -1 0 +1 +2 +3 +4 +5 +6
+7 +8 +9 +10

3) Miscellaneous

_____

-10 -9 -8 -7 -6 -5 -4 -3 -2 -1 0 +1 +2 +3 +4 +5 +6
+7 +8 +9 +10

For this final category, add up your three scores for a total that will be between -30 and +30. Divide this score by 3 to come up with an average Financial Resources score between -10 and +10.

Record your average score here: _____
Date: _____

SET NUMBER FOUR

Principle I

Physical, Mental, Emotional and Spiritual Wellness

The better and more complete your physical, mental, emotional and spiritual health becomes, the greater the measure of happiness you will achieve in life. When our lives are plagued by chronic illnesses, and aches and pains, or if we happen to be constantly vulnerable to the common cold or other ailments, our morale deteriorates and so does our delight in life.

Being constantly out of sorts is often the result of some physical problems that can easily be remedied. The worst thing to do is to do nothing. The first thing we ought to do is to get a proper medical diagnosis. If nothing can be done to relieve a medical issue, then our task is to learn to accept that which cannot be changed, to adapt to some limitations of our activity level, and eventually compensate for those limitations in other areas of our lives.

One example of this kind of compensation and adaptation is illustrated by the famous impressionist painter, Renoir. In his last 25 years of his active artistic life, he suffered from debilitating arthritis. His passion for painting, including 400 hundred masterpieces in his last 10 years, did not subside with his physical limitations. Instead, he tied his brushes to his hands and arms since he was unable to hold them tightly. He also found and developed sophisticated ways to access his easels.

Another much younger artist became extremely depressed all the way to the point of considering suicide. He had found out that his severe retinal deterioration was going to prevent him from finishing 25 paintings that he was scheduled to show in a local art gallery. Therapeutic intervention helped him to realize that he could still enjoy a few more months of his artistic creativity rather than focus on the quantity of paintings he could produce.

Yet another example of this phenomenon was demonstrated by a personal patient of mine. He was a very bright man in his mid-fifties, but he was becoming very depressed as he realized he could no longer run his normal five miles every morning. Through some short term individual therapy, he was able to accept the fact that some physiological changes had gradually occurred. He also discovered that 2 miles of daily jogging could be just as enjoyable and with a lot less pain. He had the option to lament and get more depressed, but instead he refused to give in to his gradually worsening limitations.

Following the instructions provided in the last section, it is time to rate yourself on the following elements that affect your general wellness.

A. Physical Health

1) Diet

-10 -9 -8 -7 -6 -5 -4 -3 -2 -1 0 +1 +2 +3 +4 +5 +6 +7 +8 +9 +10

Do you eat a balanced diet? How often do you indulge in "junk food"? Does your diet include fruits? Green vegetables? Excessive amounts of meat? Do you use excessive amounts of caffeine? Artificial sweeteners? Tobacco? Appetite suppressants?

Why did you rate yourself the way you did about your diet?

_____
_____

_____
_____

_____
_____

2) Weight control

_____

-10 -9 -8 -7 -6 -5 -4 -3 -2 -1 0 $+1$ $+2$ $+3$ $+4$ $+5$ $+6$ $+7$ $+8$ $+9$ $+10$

Do you stay within your recommended weight range according to your gender, age, height and general build? Do you normally use appetite suppressants? Diuretics? Thyroid medications? Have you tried crash diets? Fad diets?

Your self-evaluation is based on the following:

_____
_____

_____
_____

_____
_____

175

3) Exercise

-10 -9 -8 -7 -6 -5 -4 -3 -2 -1 0 +1 +2 +3 +4 +5 +6 +7 +8 +9 +10

Are you involved in a regular fitness program? Is it on your own? Supervised by fitness professionals? Do you do any sports or physical activities on a routine basis for fun?

Your self-evaluation is based on the following:

_____
_____

_____
_____

_____
_____

B. Mental, Emotional Health

_____

-10 -9 -8 -7 -6 -5 -4 -3 -2 -1 0 +1 +2 +3 +4 +5 +6
+7 +8 +9 +10

How do you handle anxiety, depression, stress, or significant crises in your life? How do you handle things such as major unexpected illnesses, death, divorce, separation, or financial insecurity?

Your self-evaluation and rating are based on:

_____
_____

_____
_____

_____
_____

177

C. Spiritual health

-10 -9 -8 -7 -6 -5 -4 -3 -2 -1 0 +1 +2 +3 +4 +5 +6
+7 +8 +9 +10

Are you comfortable with your beliefs or absence of beliefs in a higher power? What have you done and/or what can you do to reach your own comfort level? Do you accept and respect religious beliefs different than your own?

Your rating is based on the following:

_____
_____

_____
_____

_____
_____

Principle II

Knowledge

An ignorant person may believe that he is truly happy. However, according to most learned people, an ignorant person is not truly happy since he is unaware of the immense possibilities for happiness that only a well-educated and knowledgeable person can experience. Humans are curious organisms by nature. Knowledge helps to satisfy curiosity about one's own self, about the world, and the universe in which we live. The better and more complete one's education, the greater measure of happiness that person should be able to achieve.

The Greek philosopher Plato defined knowledge as "justified true beliefs." Einstein said that culture is what we are left with when we have forgotten everything we learned in school.

Knowledge is actually an extremely vast concept. It is a sense of awareness with oneself, others and numerous concepts through various disciplines, mostly acquired through education. This education may be obtained in school or through formal academic institutions, or it can be self-taught through research or even through exposure to major and significant life events.

-10 -9 -8 -7 -6 -5 -4 -3 -2 -1 0 +1 +2 +3 +4 +5 +6 +7 +8 +9 +10

How would you score your overall level of knowledge? How did you acquire it? What means are you using to improve that level?

179

Why did you score yourself the way that you did?

_____
_____
_____
_____
_____
_____

Principle III

Social Wellness

Humans are social creatures by nature. We are not designed to be recluses or hermits. The better and more complete one's social involvement and relationships become, such as romances, friendships, or social networking, the more you will develop socially. Increased social development and adaptability lead to a greater measure of overall happiness.

4) Comfort zone within your own skin.

_____

-10 -9 -8 -7 -6 -5 -4 -3 -2 -1 0 +1 +2 +3 +4 +5 +6 +7 +8 +9 +10

How comfortable are you with the way you look? Do you feel like others judge you negatively based on your appearance?

Examples of negative scores were demonstrated by a patient I met as a young woman. She was anorexic and very proud of the fact that her mother bought her clothing from the children's department. Another very attractive female patient of mine was still searching for the most famous plastic surgeons to assist her with her 6th or 7th facial surgery.

Why did you rate yourself the way you did?

_____
_____

_____
_____

_____
_____

2) Intimacy

_____
_____

-10 -9 -8 -7 -6 -5 -4 -3 -2 -1 0 +1 +2 +3 +4 +5 +6 +7 +8 +9 +10

This indicator is seen by some as pleasurable if not wonderful. By others, it could be perceived as a duty, or even as a sinful act or a conjugal obligation. Rate your experience as positive, negative, or as one of indifference. Intimacy can even be experienced in ways other than sexual – such as spiritual or intellectual intimacy.

181

This is a delicate subject which is often embarrassing to discuss openly. This can be true even if you have reached a good level of intimacy with your significant other.

What are the reasons that you graded yourself as you did?

_____
_____

_____
_____

_____
_____

3) Social Life

_____

-10 -9 -8 -7 -6 -5 -4 -3 -2 -1 0 +1 +2 +3 +4 +5 +6 +7 +8 +9 +10

To what extent are you satisfied with your social life? Do you have a lot of friends? Do you attend social events? Are you involved in online communities? What have you done or are you planning to do to reach a good level of satisfaction?

Explain the reasons for your rating.

_____
_____

_____
_____

_____
_____

4) Social Adaptability

_____
_____

-10 -9 -8 -7 -6 -5 -4 -3 -2 -1 0 +1 +2 +3 +4
          +5 +6 +7 +8 +9 +10

When you move into a new neighborhood, town, state, or even a new country - do you find meeting new people with different backgrounds a pleasant or a difficult experience?

I remember a patient of mine who was extremely unhappy after having to move away from her home state of Pennsylvania to Arizona. She did so because her husband got an excellent job opportunity in Arizona. After several months of unsuccessful therapy for his wife, the husband had no other resources but to move back to the East Coast. There was no way for this woman to be truly happy in Arizona due a deficiency in social adaptability.

183

Now explain why you gave yourself the score that you did:

_____

_____

_____

_____

_____

_____

Principle IV

Character Building

"Character" refers to the total sum of traits that make up your personality. People who have low self-esteem, who feel that lack of intrinsic value, or who wish they could be someone else are generally unhappy. Most people want to be considered individuals of good character. Some of the traits that people value in themselves and in others are listed below as areas to score yourself.

Let us keep in mind that character-building is a lifelong process that requires focus and persistence. There are many components to character building. A well-built character includes a sound moral code, but it also refers to the totality of traits that make up a well-rounded person. These traits may include being educated, accomplished, and comfortable in many social settings and situations. A person with strong character will be a person with healthy self-esteem obtained by the development of one's integrity, authenticity, kindness, compassion, respect for others, tolerance and many other related qualities.

1) Authenticity

-10 -9 -8 -7 -6 -5 -4 -3 -2 -1 0 +1 +2 +3 +4 +5 +6 +7 +8 +9 +10

This is a state of being which is developed through consistent presentation of oneself, in which motives, deeds and claims are square with the truth. .

Does this following anecdote reveal a man who practices authenticity or deception? A wealthy merchant wanted a tax write-off but he also wanted to receive recognition and credit for being a philanthropist. He therefore donated a large sum of money to fund the building of a safe house for women. At the ribbon-cutting ceremony, he was asked to say a few words. In his speech, he alluded to his monetary gift as having been more than he could really afford, but he nevertheless went forward with his contribution on the grounds that he knew that women were in greater need of the safe house than he was in need of expanding his company. Was he being authentic – or deceptive?

Now write down the reasons for your rating of yourself:

_____
_____

_____
_____

_____
_____

2) Compassion, Kindness, Understanding of Others' Needs

_____
                              _____

-10 -9 -8 -7 -6 -5 -4 -3 -2 -1 0 +1 +2 +3 +4 +5 +6
                +7 +8 +9 +10

Compassion is a feeling of empathy for others that allows us to share their suffering and motivates our desire to help others. Compassion could be easily felt when sharing the same background (ethnic, religious, nationality). Compassion can also be expressed through donations to charitable organizations for a specific cause such as a natural disaster. Volunteering is another way to show compassion and interest in helping others in need.

Why did you rate yourself the way you did?

_____
_____

_____
_____

_____
_____

3) Integrity, Self-Honesty

_____

-10 -9 -8 -7 -6 -5 -4 -3 -2 -1 0 +1 +2 +3 +4 +5 +6
+7 +8 +9 +10

This refers to another set of strong moral principles. Integrity can also be defined as rectitude, probity, or truthfulness. Integrity has been defined as 'what one does when no-one else is watching.'

So why did you score yourself the way that you did?

_____

_____

_____

_____

_____

_____

4) Virtue

_____

-10 -9 -8 -7 -6 -5 -4 -3 -2 -1 0 +1 +2 +3 +4 +5 +6
+7 +8 +9 +10

Today most people define "virtue" as simply moral excellence. Aristotle, however, defined a virtue as being at a point between a deficiency and an excess of a character trait. A virtue is a positive trait or quality deemed to be morally just and therefore valued as a foundation of the principles and good moral being. Personal virtues are valued as promoting collective and individual greatness. In short, "virtue" is the collective essence of one's total personality.

189

What are the reasons of rating yourself the way you did?

_____
_____

_____
_____

_____
_____

Principle V

Financial Resources

Financial resources are often referred to when describing the ability to obtain food, clothing, and shelter. Others include transportation means, recreation, and even health care when talking about financial resources. However, according to Aristotle, adequate financial resources are important for many other reasons. For example, finances could be a way to obtain a more adequate education, to attend trade schools, or to get closer to reaching a middle class status.

Once again, the better and more complete one is able to obtain the above (food, shelter, clothing, transportation, health care, recreation, education, and the means to develop one's cherished talents and special gifts), the greater level of happiness he will be able to reach.

Rate yourself on the financial resources to obtain the following.

4) Basic necessities, which include food, clothing, and shelter.

-10 -9 -8 -7 -6 -5 -4 -3 -2 -1 0 +1 +2 +3 +4 +5 +6 +7 +8 +9 +10

Can you afford to eat healthy foods and have a balance diet? Can you afford proper clothing adequate for different seasons? Is your habitat safe and sound and in a decent neighborhood? You could even include proper transportation means in this rating.

Your reasons to rate yourself as you did:

_____
_____

_____
_____

_____
_____

2) Adequate Health Care

$$-10 \ -9 \ -8 \ -7 \ -6 \ -5 \ -4 \ -3 \ -2 \ -1 \ 0 \ +1 \ +2 \ +3 \ +4 \ +5 \ +6$$
$$+7 \ +8 \ +9 \ +10$$

Adequate health care often means being able to afford the proper medical insurance or coverage (private insurance companies, Veteran's Administration benefits, Social Security,) having access to primary care physicians and being near specialists if needed. Do you have access to hospitals, hospices, laboratory facilities and surgical procedures?

Why did you rate yourself the way you did?

_____

_____

_____

_____

_____

_____

3) Miscellaneous

-10 -9 -8 -7 -6 -5 -4 -3 -2 -1 0 +1 +2 +3 +4 +5 +6
+7 +8 +9 +10

This could refer to having the means to allow your natural talents to develop and reach their full potential. An artistic wood carver or a gifted musician should be able to purchase the proper tools and instruments needed to perform in these privileged areas of expertise. Another gifted individual should be able to further his education, return or start college, or get into doctorate or fellowship programs

What are the reasons for rating yourself the way you did?

_____

_____

_____

_____

_____

_____

Summary Chart

Now it is time to come up with an overall average score for each of the above-described categories. Copy forward your scores for each of the following:

<u>Physical, Mental, Emotional and Spiritual Wellness</u>

16) Diet

_____

-10 -9 -8 -7 -6 -5 -4 -3 -2 -1 0 +1 +2 +3 +4 +5 +6
        +7 +8 +9 +10

17) Weight Control

_____

-10 -9 -8 -7 -6 -5 -4 -3 -2 -1 0 +1 +2 +3 +4 +5 +6
        +7 +8 +9 +10

18) Exercise

_____

-10 -9 -8 -7 -6 -5 -4 -3 -2 -1 0 +1 +2 +3 +4 +5 +6
        +7 +8 +9 +10

19) Mental and Emotional Health

_____

-10 -9 -8 -7 -6 -5 -4 -3 -2 -1 0 +1 +2 +3 +4 +5 +6
        +7 +8 +9 +10

195

20) Spiritual Health

-10 -9 -8 -7 -6 -5 -4 -3 -2 -1 0 +1 +2 +3 +4 +5 +6 +7 +8 +9 +10

Now add up your scores for these five categories. Your total score will be somewhere between -50 and +50. Divide that total score by 5 to find out your average score for Physical, Mental, Emotional and Spiritual Wellness that will be between -10 and +10.

Record your average score here: _____
Date: _____

Knowledge

13) Knowledge

-10 -9 -8 -7 -6 -5 -4 -3 -2 -1 0 +1 +2 +3 +4 +5 +6 +7 +8 +9 +10

Since there is only one score in the 'Knowledge' category, this number will also be your average score.

Record your average score here: _____
Date: _____

Social Wellness

1) Comfort Zone

_____
          _____
-10 -9 -8 -7 -6 -5 -4 -3 -2 -1 0 +1 +2 +3 +4 +5 +6
                  +7 +8 +9 +10

14) Intimacy

_____
          _____
-10 -9 -8 -7 -6 -5 -4 -3 -2 -1 0 +1 +2 +3 +4 +5 +6
                  +7 +8 +9 +10

15) Social Life

_____
          _____
-10 -9 -8 -7 -6 -5 -4 -3 -2 -1 0 +1 +2 +3 +4 +5 +6 +7 +8 +9
                    +10

16) Social Adaptability

_____
          _____
-10 -9 -8 -7 -6 -5 -4 -3 -2 -1 0 +1 +2 +3 +4 +5 +6 +7 +8 +9
                    +10

Your total score for these four categories should fall between -40 and + 40. Divide that total score by 4 in order to reach an average score for Social Wellness between -10 and +10.

Record your average score here: _____
Date: _____

<u>Character Building</u>

1) Authenticity

_____
          _____
 -10 -9 -8 -7 -6 -5 -4 -3 -2 -1 0 +1 +2 +3 +4 +5 +6
                +7 +8 +9 +10

2) Compassion, Kindness, Understanding of Others' Needs

_____

-10 -9 -8 -7 -6 -5 -4 -3 -2 -1 0 +1 +2 +3 +4 +5 +6
                    +7 +8 +9 +10

3) Integrity, Self-Honesty

_____

-10 -9 -8 -7 -6 -5 -4 -3 -2 -1 0 +1 +2 +3 +4 +5 +6
                    +7 +8 +9 +10

4) Virtue

_____

-10 -9 -8 -7 -6 -5 -4 -3 -2 -1 0 +1 +2 +3 +4 +5 +6
                    +7 +8 +9 +10

Once again, add up your four totals for this category for a total
between -40 and +40. Divide this number by 4 to find your
average score for Character Building which will be between -
10 and +10.

Record your average score here: _____
Date: _____

Financial Resources

1) Basic Necessities

_____

-10 -9 -8 -7 -6 -5 -4 -3 -2 -1 0 +1 +2 +3 +4 +5 +6
+7 +8 +9 +10

2) Adequate Health Care

_____

-10 -9 -8 -7 -6 -5 -4 -3 -2 -1 0 +1 +2 +3 +4 +5 +6
+7 +8 +9 +10

3) Miscellaneous

_____

-10 -9 -8 -7 -6 -5 -4 -3 -2 -1 0 +1 +2 +3 +4 +5 +6
+7 +8 +9 +10

For this final category, add up your three scores for a total that will be between -30 and +30. Divide this score by 3 to come up with an average Financial Resources score between -10 and +10.

Record your average score here: _____
Date: _____

Part Three
Coping Skills and Strategies
£

The Importance of Coping Skills and Strategies

So far we have been taking inventory of things we do well, things we do poorly, and things we do not do at all to achieve our desired level of wellness and happiness; however, we have said very little of how to bring about the level of happiness and wellness that we desire. Coping skills help us to manage our lives in such a way as to bring about the goals we set for ourselves.

"Coping Skills" are tools to manage dysfunctional behaviors and unmanageable feelings that make it seem that your life is out of control

Many books on self-assessment or self-help deal with analysis but do not then teach or show you how to cope with dysfunctional problems in your life. There are key elements in learning how to identify problems, how to be in awareness of the parts of your life that are unmanageable, how to identify unhealthy patterns and habits that continue to be destructive to you, and how to problem-solve or find solutions that assist you in developing skills to understand, and to manage or change those difficult areas in your life.

No person is born already knowing how to successfully manage difficult feelings and their resulting behaviors. As children, we are dependent on our primary caregivers to instruct us how to manage our emotions and their subsequent reactions. Some of us are fortunate enough to have knowledgeable caregivers that teach us positive and healthy ways to manage our feelings and behaviors. They are able to provide constructive, safe, and nurturing techniques for us to successfully accomplish life goals.

Some caregivers are themselves not informed and are then unable to provide beneficial information to help their children problem solve their own issues. They are unable to teach constructive or safe and nurturing pathways in critical areas. Some caregivers are even destructive or harmful to themselves and latter, by example, teach unhealthy and damaging ways to react to difficult issues. Their damaging examples are disrespectful, wounding, or demeaning, and they leave feelings of a helpless lack of control in their wake.

The good news is that as adults, we are no longer dependent up on caregivers to care for us. We do not have to be subject to the dysfunctional or hurtful teachings of others. We can learn how to succeed in building a constructive and healthy way of living for ourselves where we can feel good about who we are and about our relationships with others. We have a right to happiness and experience joy in living. It requires work, learning, and practicing new skills in daily life to define what works best for you to help build the kind of life that you want to have.

Coping skills are the tools that we develop as an approach to identify and solve problems and to recognize when it is necessary to go for help, such as going to a doctor or professional therapist. Coping skills help us learn to practice self-discipline in certain areas, how to recognize negative patterns of behavior, how to understand where unhealthy behaviors came from, and how to replace unhealthy behaviors with ones that are positive and constructive for you.

Without coping skills, we can find ourselves floundering and unable to move forward in accomplishing the goals that we have set for ourselves to build a productive and fulfilling existence. It may be that we can identify many areas in our lives that could use improvement–but without coping strategies, we will struggle to make positive changes in these areas.

Coping skills are the tools you will need in your life "tool box" to teach yourself healthier ways to improve and live your life.

Coping skills can be viewed as physical, mental, or emotional. Physical coping skills could include using a medically approved smoking device to help stop smoking. An example of a mental coping skill could be recognition that the events surrounding us are not healthy and choosing to leave an unhealthy environment. Emotional coping skills help us to recognize emotions such as degrees of sadness, happiness, or anger.

Common traits of coping skills include the following:

1.   Coping skills are universal and available to anyone who wishes to develop them.

2.   Some coping skills are learned from an individual's culture, some are learned from care givers, some are passed down in families and from peers, some are grounded in religious teachings and educational programs, and some are founded in civic groups.

3.   Coping skills allow for personal application and can be customized to meet each individual's needs and the problems they face. For example, if you find that yelling is unsafe for you in your own home (your safe place) because yelling triggers past trauma issues, then you can make it a rule that yelling is allowed ONLY outside of your home. Your job is to communicate to all concerned what is necessary for you in your environment to feel safe.

4. Coping skills are aids we develop to produce healthy outcomes; they are building blocks for us and are intended to help us create a better life.

5. Intuition is important. Every person is intuitive in differing areas of their lives. Coming to know where it is that you are intuitive, following your intuitive markers and acting upon them may save you from danger. Intuition is a coping skill in itself and should not be ignored. However, as with all other types of coping skills listed here, the outcomes must square with results that are positive and are real.

6. New coping skills, especially, must be tested out in day to day living experiences and be found to be successful before we will change old coping skills that we are accustomed to using.

7. Coping skills require continual adjustment to meet changing needs.

Coping mechanisms should not be confused with pseudo-coping skills or unhealthy or negative habits, such as using alcohol to reduce anxiety or to sleep. These types of "coping" mechanisms prove destructive in the long run, are insidious, and eventually can cause illness, injury, or even death. Unhealthy coping skills cause harm and are a big "red flag" that requires immediate attention.

Defining your coping skills takes some thought. It is important to know what skills you already have. Once these are understood, it becomes easier to identify the unique pattern of issues in your life that you have created. By writing your issues down as problems, looking at what actions or coping skills you have already used to correct these problems, and understanding the overall outcome of your problem solutions, you will be able to see if you have the right tools in your life tool box to be successful in managing the issue. If you have learned to create appropriate coping skills to address the issue, the outcome of the problem is usually successful; conversely, if the coping skills you use are ineffective, you are likely to find yourself unsuccessful and frustrated in problem resolution.

Personalizing Your Coping Skills

Let us look at some areas in your life where you may need some additional tools. Look at each dimension you have scored in Part One. First, pay attention to those scores that indicate you are satisfied with a particular part of your life. Look at each element within the dimension and list those coping skills that you can identify that you believe have been helpful in your success. Record your responses in the "Coping Skills Log" found at the end of this section. Second, look at the scores in each dimension that indicate you are not satisfied with this area of your life. Look at each element within the dimension and write down the coping skills you feel you have used to assist you. Can you identify at least three? If these skills you identified did not work, can you state why they did not work? Write them down. Third, can you identify any negative coping skills in any of these areas? Remember, negative coping skills are those types of skills that may meet our immediate needs but cause us harm in the long run such as lying our way out of an issue because we do not know how to handle conflict and eventually being labeled by ourselves or others as a "fabricator." Write down these identified negative coping skills and set them aside.

You will be surprised that the coping skills you identify (positive and negative) are skills you probably use in multiple situations on a regular basis. You want to learn how to build your skills to work for you in managing your life, to enhance your self-esteem, and to increase confidence in yourself and relationships with others.

207

How does one develop appropriate coping skills that will work? First, you need to identify and evaluate those coping skills you already use to problem-solve issues that present themselves on a daily basis. You will find that some of the coping tools you use are successful and some are not. Knowing what coping skills you have that work and do not work makes it easier to identify and respond to life's challenges successfully and to correct unsuccessful or harmful coping methods that routinely do not meet your needs. If you do not feel you know what skills you already have you can discover them easily by writing them down when they occur.

Second, you want to know what coping skills you actually used to handle the problem. What did you DO or what ACTION did you take to handle the issue or problem? Write it down in the "Problem Solution" section in the Coping Skills Log at the end of this section. Looking at what you actually have done (or not done) to address the issues in your life is an eye-opening event.

Third, ask yourself if the action you took was successful or constructive for you in solving the problem. Ask yourself why or why not. Did the action produce the outcome that you wanted? If the answer is yes, then the action you took to solve the problem is a positive coping skill. If the outcome was not successful, you need to look at the issue at hand more closely and develop additional, different, or new coping skills. You may be surprised to find how you routinely use the same coping skills over and over without success to address different challenges. Writing them down is helpful in better understanding of how many and what kind of tools you have in your personal tool box and where it is that you need to develop more tools.

New tools come from a variety of places and once discovered have to be tested out in day to day life to see if, when applied, they will work and become a coping skill that is beneficial to you. Tools are found in such places as research, media, many sites on the internet, peers, and educational programs and are implemented and fine-tuned through at least some trial and error experience. Remember, no one is born automatically knowing how to rebuild a carburetor of a car, how to be successful in their relationships, or how to change difficult behaviors or accept their own or others' vulnerabilities or strengths. These skills, once acquired, provide us with the correct information to manage life events. If a certain skill has worked for others in addressing an issue, you will know only if it works for you by testing it out, on a conscious level, to see if indeed it does work and is producing the outcome you want. If it produces the outcome you want you will automatically put this new tool in your tool box and use it again.

Acquiring effective skills may sound difficult but the benefits are definitely workable and worthwhile.

Practicing Coping Skills To Improve Your Life

So how can you practice your coping skills? Some coping skills are automatic and often occur out of our awareness. Each time we address a problem we use a set of coping skills to find solutions and if the solutions work we move on to the many other demands we have requiring our attention. If the coping skills do not work then we search for other coping skills that do work or develop all together new coping skills.

Developing new coping practices are not as easy for us because they require trial and error application to see if they are going to meet our needs. Changing ineffective coping skills that are habitual is difficult to do; it's like a bad habit and takes some time to break. Practicing specific coping skills happens in everyday living within a time frame that is based on how difficult the problem is and whether our emotional self and our intellectual self are able to respond in a parallel fashion. For example, a person may know that it is not healthy to smoke and that smoking is a health hazard. They may want to quit smoking. However, emotionally and physically it is very difficult for them to stop smoking. Practicing methods to stop smoking may take a person several days, weeks, months or even years. The more the issue is within people's awareness and the more they use coping skills to address the problems surrounding the issue, the more likely they will have a positive outcome. So, how often must everyone practice coping skills? As long as it takes to solve the problem constructively.

When Do You Ask For Professional Help?

So how do you know if you need professional help? The easy answer is any time you are in danger of hurting yourself or someone else physically, mentally, or emotionally. Once you have crossed a line in hurting yourself or others, it is very easy and almost predictable that you will immediately go to that line and cross it again or up the ante the next time you are faced with similar circumstances. Hurting yourself or others is abusive and demeaning. There are many reasons why people hurt themselves or others, and any of these reasons require intervention. Hurting yourself or others is a warning sign that help in developing effective coping skills is urgently needed. We, as adults, are our own caregivers and as such can take responsibility for our own level of care. We may not know how to but, we can learn and can ask for help when needed. When your safety or the safety of others is as risk, you should seek immediate help.

There are many places one can go for help. In case of life or death issues, call 911 or your local emergency number. In other situations, help is found by contacting law enforcement, your doctor (medical or psychiatric), counselors, hot lines, self-help groups such as Alcoholics Anonymous, Narcotic Anonymous, Overeaters Anonymous, Gamblers Anonymous, Al-Anon, parenting classes, anger management classes, or other appropriate groups. Doing nothing could have tragic results.

211

Appreciate Your Progress

You will then need to test out what you learn in your day to day living to see if it is successful for you. When you trust that what you have learned is working better than what you were doing before, you will change your behavior and your vision of yourself.

Working on yourself and the issues in your life is another way one builds self-esteem. Self-esteem derives from the things we do to make us feel good about ourselves. Conversely, low self-esteem is a failure to do those things which lift our hearts, our spirits, and our feelings about our lives. When we are living our lives in a manner that meets our innermost ethical values and these values are based on wholeness and healthy outcomes, we feel successful and good about ourselves. It is best not to beat ourselves up when we fall short of meeting our expectations. Instead, we identify what is amiss and work toward correcting the problem. When we are critical or set unrealistic expectations and standards for ourselves or others, we are not respecting ourselves or the people around us. It is much harder to identify the problem, and we often feel defeated with little energy or stimulus to correct the problem. Learning to build constructive coping skills that are workable in our lives gives us the tools to manage adversity, despair, personal hardships, and the feeling that life is not worth living. The tools in coping skills allow us to work effectively and efficiently toward meeting our expectations. We feel more confident and competent in the realization that life can be joyful without feeling guilty about being happy.

In summary, defining your problems and expending an honest amount of effort to correct them will bring you a noticeable measure of well- being and satisfaction in your life. Periodic review of issues and outcomes will help you to keep on track towards maintaining and improving your coping skills and therefore your sense of well-being. Equally important are your efforts to discover new problems and the appropriate methodology of managing them. This must be done in order to keep your program vital, vibrant, and alive.

Incorporating The Right Coping Skills
Into Your Daily Life

The following tool can be recorded in your daily journal or in the following work sheets and logs.

The first two work sheets ask you to identify (1) those coping skills you believe you already have that are positive and work for you and (2) those that are negative and do not provide the expected result you want. The third page of the coping skills' log is intended for you to write out daily problems, the actions you take to solve them, and if the action you took to manage them was successful or not.

It is important that you use the work logs for one to three week(s) on a daily basis to gather enough information. You will find that you have any number of problems that repeat themselves in your daily living in differing scenarios. The same problems will reoccur over and over in different situations if not addressed or solved, You will begin to see a pattern forming showing how you identify or interpret the problems, your reactions or actions, and the resulting outcomes. You will see which coping skills you have used that were successful. You will also see where you can use the same skills in similar scenarios. Look at each dimension and those areas that continue to be a problems without solutions. These are the areas you need new or improved coping skills. Explore other avenues to determine what you believe you would be willing to test out as a new and constructive coping skill to address the problem. Test it out. If there is a particular area in your life where you are "stuck," try asking for help. Have fun with self-learning. You will be delighted when you discover that you actually can COPE.

Note: The Coping Skills' work sheets begin on the page immediately following the Post Script.

Post Script

£

The program presented in this book has been written to help you significantly improve your health and happiness. If you will follow this program with perseverance, determination, and total self-honesty, you will find that your level of success will improve significantly. If you do not, your efforts will fail. We reap what we sow. Your commitment to complete this work can only improve your life and bring you a greater measure joy and appreciation of the opportunities that life offers.

Coping Skills Work Sheets

Name:_____

     Date:_____

Identified Effective or Positive Coping Skills: Why were they effective or positive?

_____
_____

_____
_____

_____
_____

_____
_____

_____
_____

_____
_____

Identified Ineffective or Negative Coping Skills: Why were they ineffective or negative?

_____
_____

_____
_____

_____
_____

_____
_____

_____
_____

_____
_____

Week One: Coping Skills Work Log

Problem:

_____

_____

Action taken to solve the problem:

_____

Outcome of action taken:

_____

Was the outcome successful?

_____

Why or why not?

_____

_____

Problem:

_____

_____

Action taken to solve the problem:

_____

Outcome of action taken:

_____

Was the outcome successful?

_____

Why or why not?

_____

_____

Problem:

_____

_____

Action taken to solve the problem:

_____

Outcome of action taken:

_____

_____

Was the outcome successful?

_____

Why or why not?

_____

_____

Problem:

_____

_____

Action taken to solve the problem:

_____

Outcome of action taken:

_____

_____

Was the outcome successful?

_____

Why or why not?

_____

_____

Problem:

_____

_____

Action taken to solve the problem:

_____

Outcome of action taken:

_____

_____

Was the outcome successful?

_____

Why or why not?

_____

_____

Problem:

_____

_____

Action taken to solve the problem:

_____

Outcome of action taken:

_____

_____

Was the outcome successful?

_____

Why or why not?

_____

_____

Problem:

_____

_____

Action taken to solve the problem:

_____

Outcome of action taken:

_____

_____

Was the outcome successful?

_____

Why or why not?

_____

_____

Problem:

_____

_____

Action taken to solve the problem:

_____

Outcome of action taken:

_____

_____

Was the outcome successful?

_____

Why or why not?

_____

_____

Problem:

_____

_____

Action taken to solve the problem:

_____

Outcome of action taken:

_____

_____

Was the outcome successful?

_____

223

Why or why not?

_____

_____

Problem:

_____

_____

Action taken to solve the problem:

_____

Outcome of action taken:

_____

_____

Was the outcome successful?

_____

Why or why not?

_____

_____

Week Two: Coping Skills Work Log

Problem:

_____

_____

Action taken to solve the problem:

_____

Outcome of action taken:

_____

_____

Was the outcome successful?

_____

Why or why not?

_____

_____

Problem:

_____

_____

Action taken to solve the problem:

_____

Outcome of action taken:

_____

_____

Was the outcome successful?

_____

Why or why not?

_____

_____

Problem:

_____

_____

Action taken to solve the problem:

_____

Outcome of action taken:

_____

_____

Was the outcome successful?

_____

Why or why not?

_____

_____

Problem:

_____

_____

Action taken to solve the problem:

_____

Outcome of action taken:

_____

_____

Was the outcome successful?

_____

Why or why not?

_____

_____

Problem:

_____

_____

Action taken to solve the problem:

_____

Outcome of action taken:

_____

_____

Was the outcome successful?

_____

Why or why not?

_____

_____

Problem:

_____

_____

Action taken to solve the problem:

_____

Outcome of action taken:

_____

_____

Was the outcome successful?

_____

Why or why not?

_____

_____

Problem:

_____

_____

Action taken to solve the problem:

_____

Outcome of action taken:

_____

_____

Was the outcome successful?

_____

Why or why not?

_____

_____

Problem:

_____

_____

Action taken to solve the problem:

_____

Outcome of action taken:

_____

_____

Was the outcome successful?

_____

Why or why not?

_____

_____

Problem:

_____

_____

Action taken to solve the problem:

_____

Outcome of action taken:

_____

_____

Was the outcome successful?

_____

Why or why not?

_____

_____

Problem:

_____

_____

Action taken to solve the problem:

_____

Outcome of action taken:

_____

_____

Was the outcome successful?

_____

231

Why or why not?

_____

_____

Problem:

_____

_____

Action taken to solve the problem:

_____

Outcome of action taken:

_____

_____

Was the outcome successful?

_____

Why or why not?

_____

_____

Problem:

_____

_____

Action taken to solve the problem:

_____

Outcome of action taken:

_____

_____

Was the outcome successful?

_____

Why or why not?

_____

_____

Problem:

_____

_____

Action taken to solve the problem:

_____

Outcome of action taken:

_____

_____

Was the outcome successful?

_____

Why or why not?

_____

_____

Problem:

_____

_____

Action taken to solve the problem:

_____

233

Outcome of action taken:

_____

_____

Was the outcome successful?

_____

Why or why not?

_____

_____

Problem:

_____

_____

Action taken to solve the problem:

_____

Outcome of action taken:

_____

_____

Was the outcome successful?

_____

Why or why not?

_____

_____

Problem:

_____

_____

Action taken to solve the problem:

_____

Outcome of action taken:

_____

_____

Was the outcome successful?

_____

Why or why not?

_____

_____

Problem:

_____

_____

Action taken to solve the problem:

_____

Outcome of action taken:

_____

_____

Was the outcome successful?

_____

Why or why not?

_____

_____

Problem:

_____

_____

Action taken to solve the problem:

_____

Outcome of action taken:

_____

_____

Was the outcome successful?

_____

Why or why not?

_____

_____

Problem:

_____

_____

Action taken to solve the problem:

_____

Outcome of action taken:

_____

_____

Was the outcome successful?

_____

Why or why not?

_____

_____

Problem:

_____

_____

Action taken to solve the problem:

_____

Outcome of action taken:

_____

_____

Was the outcome successful?

_____

Why or why not?

_____

_____

237

Problem:

_____

_____

Action taken to solve the problem:

_____

Outcome of action taken:

_____

_____

Was the outcome successful?

_____

Why or why not?

_____

_____

Week Three: Coping Skills Work Log

Problem:

_____

_____

Action taken to solve the problem:

_____

Outcome of action taken:

_____

_____

Was the outcome successful?

_____

Why or why not?

_____

_____

Problem:

_____

_____

Action taken to solve the problem:

_____

Outcome of action taken:

_____

_____

Was the outcome successful?

_____

239

Why or why not?

_____

_____

Problem:

_____

_____

Action taken to solve the problem:

_____

Outcome of action taken:

_____

_____

Was the outcome successful?

_____

Why or why not?

_____

_____

Problem:

_____

_____

Action taken to solve the problem:

_____

Outcome of action taken:

_____

_____

Was the outcome successful?

_____

Why or why not?

_____

_____

Problem:

_____

_____

Action taken to solve the problem:

_____

Outcome of action taken:

_____

_____

Was the outcome successful?

_____

Why or why not?

_____

_____

Problem:

_____

_____

241

Action taken to solve the problem:

_____

Outcome of action taken:

_____

_____

Was the outcome successful?

_____

Why or why not?

_____

_____

Problem:

_____

_____

Action taken to solve the problem:

_____

Outcome of action taken:

_____

_____

Was the outcome successful?

_____

Why or why not?

_____

_____

Problem:

_____

_____

Action taken to solve the problem:

_____

Outcome of action taken:

_____

_____

Was the outcome successful?

_____

Why or why not?

_____

_____

Problem:

_____

_____

Action taken to solve the problem:

_____

Outcome of action taken:

_____

_____

Was the outcome successful?

_____

Why or why not?

_____

_____

243

Problem:

_____

_____

Action taken to solve the problem:

_____

Outcome of action taken:

_____

Was the outcome successful?

_____

Why or why not?

_____

THE END

www.ingramcontent.com/pod-product-compliance
Lightning Source LLC
Chambersburg PA
CBHW062110090426
42741CB00016B/3384